seniors in *Love*

A Second Chance for Single, Divorced and Widowed Seniors

Robert Wolley

Hatala Geroproducts • Greentop, Missouri

Seniors In Love: A Second Chance for Single, Widowed,
and Divorced Seniors, by Robert Wolley
ISBN 1-9331670-42-4
ISBN 9781933167428
LC Control no. 2005922569

Songs mentioned in this work: "Ain't We Got Fun," lyrics by Gus Kahn and Raymond B. Egan; music by Richard Whiting. "I'm Just Wild About Harry," words and music by Noble Sissle and Hubie Blake. "Carolina in the Morning" and "My Buddy," lyrics by Gus Kahn; music by Walter Donaldson. "Barney Google," words and music by Billy Rose and Con Conrad. "Hard Hearted Hanna," words and music by Jack Yellen, Milton Ager, Bob Bigelow, and Charles. Bates. "The Man I Love," "But Not for Me," and "I Got Rhythm," words by Ira Gershwin; music by George Gershwin. "Am I Blue?" lyrics by Grant Clark; music by Harry Hest. "Cuando Vuelvas a Mi," words by Oscar Hammerstein II; music by Sigmund Romberg. "Body and Soul," words by Edward Heyman, Robert Sour, and Frank Eyton; music by Johnny Green. "Dancing with Tears in My Eyes," lyrics by Al Dubin; music by Joe Burke. "Please Don't Talk About Me When I'm Gone," by Sidney Clair, Sam H. Stept and Bee Palmer "Something to Remember You By" and "I Guess I'll Have to Change My Plans," words by Howard Dietz; music by Arthur Schwartz; "Zing! Went the Strings of My Heart," words and music by James F. Hanley; "Too Marvelous for "Words," lyrics by Johnny Mercer; music by Richard A. Whiting.

Cover design: Shaun Hoffeditz
Cover photo: Mark Hatala
Composition: Paula Presley Editorial Service, Kirksville, Missouri
Interior illustrations: Twila Schofield
Printed by Thomson-Shore, Dexter, MI, USA
Body type Adobe Bembo 14/18.

Contents

In the Beginning...

This is a book for, by, and about seniors seeking and, I hope, achieving a successful second chance at romantic love, so it is only fair to explain just how this book came to be.

The idea for the book had its beginning in my attempt at a second chance and in a rather lengthy poem I wrote for myself, "Love Thoughts in a Time of Age." I knew what I was thinking, but I had to write it down, hoping to make subjective thoughts objective, as it were. Then I could examine objectively what I had written and try to convince myself (a kind of little white lie) that I was reading someone else's words, seeking the truth of them.

Ralph Waldo Emerson, a writer from an earlier generation, said that the poet's task is to "tell how it is with him." When I first read that line, I doubted the truth of it; who wants to hear someone else's trials and tribulations? Yet I've claimed many times that the poet's job is to write the rhythms of human thoughts for those who cannot, or do not, or doubt that they can say what is in their hearts. Without realizing it, through my poetry I was doing exactly what Emerson described.

Rest assured, this is not a book of poetry. You won't offend me if you skip the poem with which I open this book or the poem at the end from which most chapters flow. Of course, I'll think you shortchanged yourself if you do, but I'll never know, will I?

It has long been my habit to write out complex thoughts in longhand, thinking, organizing, and evaluating as I go along. As I write, dozens, sometimes hundreds, of examples, analogies, and metaphors jump into my head, sometimes illuminating what I have written, sometimes clouding my thoughts.

Shortly after writing "Love Thoughts In a Time of Age," I wrote the poem "The Steps of Love." Then, perhaps a year after writing those two poems, I began to organize thoughts about the many people and their situations which undoubtedly had been in the back of my mind all along and upon which I had drawn unconsciously. Even as I counseled others, I drew from relevant circumstances of people I had known in the past, thought about my own situation, and began to think about a book which would explore in simple, straightforward, and understandable terms the aspirations, successes, and failures of seniors in love.

The book went through three different lives, two of which I ended, one because it was too personal and one because it was too text-bookish. What I want to offer is a book as close to a conversation with the reader as I could manage. It is a one-sided conversation, to be sure, and not very private—more like conversing in the middle of the village square.

If I have been skillful, you will hold up your end of the conversation even if only talking back to the book. My intent is to get you thinking positive thoughts about what may be one of life's most important endeavors, your second (or maybe even first) chance to love someone and to be loved in return.

I ask that you interact with me, think about what you read—really converse as much as one can with a written text. Recently a woman sought my advice about an important step in her life. With her I began to explore the potential options and consequences. She shut me off, wanting no discussion of either. It was then I realized she was not seeking my insight or opinion; she was seeking my confirmation of her already achieved decision. I clammed up; she had made a decision and wanted only my approval. I let her rationalize her choice and told her I understood, which in truth I didn't fully. But at that point it was none of my business, and I knew she didn't want my thoughts.

You do not have to agree with my point of view or with my conclusions. I ask that you *do* think about them, weigh them, consider their relevancy for you. Accept, reject, modify; it's up to you. This book will be helpful only if it helps you think. After that, you are on your own, but not alone. For your part in an intimate senior relationship, you will determine what to do and how to go about it.

Love Thoughts
In a Time of Age

The young immortal, cute, and playful Cupid,
toys with me, his golden arrow embedded in my heart,
and as with all the gods and humans before,
intimidating passions arise, focused on the one
before whom I'd stand, myself declare,

> if I dared.

All would-be lovers are by Euripides warned:
Cupid releases his arrows in pairs.
Shot with pleasing golden arrow, I fear,
knowing not the truth, a leaded arrow lodged in her,
and instead of passion, distrust, dislike,

> revulsion.

I feel a sudden kinship, understand John Alden
and Cyrano. Neither could speak or read his intent.
Once I thought them tongue-tied, mute,
weak-kneed cowards, fearful only that
if love-sounds they released, idiot's babble

> it would be.

Now I know the truth. For golden arrow they
    hoped,
leaden arrows they feared, and if lead had entered
their desired's heart, learn it not face to face,

let messenger receive the lead–fist blow,
and if rejected, spurned, let friend tear the heart,

                       not her.

    A wise man said, "Love makes cowards of us all."
If that be so, then greatest coward am I.
I dare not speak my practiced lines
nor friend can find to present my cause.
My thoughts confined to soliloquy,

                   I say them here.

    Dark her colored halo, and through it I'd weave my
        fingers,
seeking her cheeks, let my hands rest there,
hair and hands framing her face, and eyes I'd pray seeing
        only me,
and lips unspeaking, should they be kissed,
telling me all I need to know,

                 and more.

    Or less. Ah, there's the risk.
Youth dares. Oh, to be young again,
to begin anew, to chance all,
to wager ego, the very soul of self,
that her eyes and lips and body would declare

                 affirmation.

    My mind is young, adolescent even, when all is
        possible
and images weave romantic embraces;

the heart is young, alive, beating, pounding with rhythms
      of life,
racing with vibrations caused by the thought of her.
Alas, the body fails heart and mind.
Even as the heart grows stronger, the mind keener,
the body witnesses to time,

                                    and neglect.

      What would she see? Not Apollo,
not the trained, tuned athlete of long ago,
but an old man with an old man's body,
graying, thickening, limping, on which time and neglect
      took revenge.
Do men and women think differently about such things?
Would she see beyond the girth and retreating hair
and annoying aches and pains?

                              Dare I ask?

      My body trembles with passion.
From her face, I'd let my hands explore
the curves and shape of her,
she, too, of age, though lesser victim of what age does,
wrinkles and sags, her shapeliness made less so by years.
What does it matter? She is woman, fair to my sight;
I am man. I would know the sight and smell,
the touch and sound and taste of her.

                              Ah, passion.

      I tell you true: old men and old women
ache with longing, a yearning eased only

by the touch and kiss of a lover's embrace.
Her zest, her vitality, her joy, her lust for life,
her smile, the twinkle in her eyes, her laugh
infuse my life with joy, and I love her
all the more.

   The young will laugh and gag and no matter what
claim I'm an old man with dirty thoughts.
Think they love calendar-confined,
that birthdays measure the heart's response,
that the physical is reserved for the young?
Children want their parents chaste;
parents lie and claim themselves so,
lest the children know that parents
think of breasts and male parts and entwined limbs
and all the acts that give pleasure and used to
create babies.

   Babies grow up to think passionate thoughts of their
     own,
and as they grow older, maybe they'll know
what their elders know.
And maybe they'll know a larger truth.
Two parts to this: without the wholesome touch
of flesh, love is incomplete, selfish, compromised,
its full expression stifled, frozen. Love
is reduced to lust if affection, friendship,
respect, sharing, trust, care
are absent.

How tell her this, that her happiness
comes above all else, that her happiness
will be mine? I make no excuse for what I feel;
I self-excuse the delay, avoiding the confrontation,
postponing the revelation, telling her, because I am
     afraid.
I proclaim these things to paper, pen in hand,
and have not dared to take her hand
and say aloud, so even I hear it for the first time.
                        Coward I am.

    My risk I acknowledge,
broken heart, bruised ego, stilled dreams.
The heart will heal, the ego mend.
The brain knows the truth; the heart doesn't.
Always heart and brain struggle; we live our lives
drawn to one or the other, guided by one or the other,
                        seldom both.

    The risk to her? Unwanted advances,
embarrassment, invasion of space and privacy.
How do I read her?
The little boy teases, pulls hair,
name calls, does brave albeit stupid things in her sight.
Do I do that? I'd like to call her dear, hold her hand,
climb a steep scenic bluff without puffing,
seem brave and strong, even if both are lies.
                        How?

Tender I'd be. I've learned tenderness
from the lack of it. Equal we'd be, man no better than
     woman,
woman no better than man, neither owner of the other,
neither more important than the other,
neither master nor mistress, the other less.
To her fulfillment I'd attend, and she to mine,
her happiness mine, mine hers.
In union we'd be one flesh, but always
there'd be space, no suffocating I am you,
                       you are me.

As alike as we are, we are not the same.
If we loved each other, we'd celebrate the differences
even as we shared them. Men and women are different;
it's their differences that excites them
and draws them together; it's their difference
that gives them pleasure. But more,
it's the unlikeness that proves the love,
the space provided the other's interest and growth.
Rootbound plants quickly die; confined butterflies
cannot spread their wings; they die too; without room to
     grow,
the intellect dies, and the spirit, too. Love is not about
     death;
it's about deep roots and expanded wings
                     and fulfillment.

In the present, past means nothing;
we are of the past, from the past;

we are not the past. Let the past be what it was;
there is only today and tomorrow.
Today is hope, tomorrow is dreams;
hope and dreams are all of me.
Life is not birth and death;
life is what's between
the twin nothingness.
Life is light between twin darkness.
She is my light; she expands my brightness,
her light gives meaning to sunrise and sunset.
I would tell her so, I long to tell her so,

if I dared.

There you have it, the seed from which this book grew, written in a long-ago cadence seldom heard these days. Poetic license.

It should be gender neutral, but it's not. That fault will not be repeated. But it's how it was with me once; the book itself will be more objective, yet I thought you had a right to know. Maybe I wrote or will write some words that mirror your thoughts regardless of gender. At our age, being seniors, sometimes beginnings are hard to explain. In this instance the beginning is known. It is also personal, something I share with you, for what could be more personal than the romance one seeks?

I have, however, eliminated all personal references. This is not my book; it is ours. I intrude upon your quest only to point out certain guideposts along the way, to caution you to think carefully about what you are feeling and the actions you may take.

So, here's to the love-filled lives, yours and mine, we have yet to live. May your future be filled with the light and beauty that only having someone to love can bring.

Forward!

And I mean that literally. Seniors advance—onward into the future!

You have picked up this book because you are in your sixties or beyond; you are a senior.

And you are single: widowed, divorced, or otherwise separated from your former partner, or perhaps never having partnered.

There is something missing in your life: an intimate, passionate affection, someone with whom to share life's joys and sorrows and with whom to stand arm in arm as you and he/she confront life's verities. In other words, you're missing love and a loving partner.

And you're asking if, at your age, you can be in love again, if you want to be in love again, and if so, whether you should reach out toward someone, and if you do, how does an elder behave?

You know the quick answer to the latter question: naturally.

But what is natural?

This book is for seniors who are single—and who are seeking or might seek a new someone to love, someone who will love you. The physical summer of our lives has passed; we are in the autumn of our years; that's nature's fact. If the sheer number of advancing years has signaled your defeat at the hands of old age, put this book down. There's nothing here for you.

However, if you are energized by the spark of life, if

you are capable of giving and receiving love, if you sense
the need for a life partner, if you want to share the rest of
your life with someone you trust and love, this book
might be for you—because things happen—affection
happens—love happens.

Should you love again? What do you do? How do
you behave? How do you deal with the risks? With
doubts and fears?

What goes on in these pages may lead to the discovery of a new love, even in one's advanced years, with
ideas about how one might handle the thought of loving
someone new, what one does to gain the love of that
person, and the effort and skills it takes to bring two
hearts and minds together in union.

❦ ❦ ❦

It was meant, I think, to give comfort to those of us
who, while we were aging, entertained the idea that
with age would come wisdom. We accumulated knowledge; in our advanced years we finally would be wise
enough to use that knowledge. In matters of life, it
seemed, all of us would become experts in living—and
loving.

There's a joke about what makes an expert: X equals
an unknown quantity and a spurt is a little drip. I am not
an expert in geriatrics, the biological study of aging and
the aging processes. I know what we all know, that our
generation is dramatically different from those that went
before. We live longer and healthier and more actively.
Compared to our grandparents and great grandparents,
we are a physically different species, or so it seems.

Mentally and emotionally, too. One example doesn't explain everything, but when my wife was pregnant with our second child, my aunt and uncle visited us. My uncle, overjoyed by the coming new life, hugged my aunt. To this day I remember her rebuke: "H---, stop it! We're too old for that!"

They weren't, and that's the pity. They were young, as I think about it now, in their fifties, but there it was, the Victorian (have to blame it on someone) idea that after menopause romance and eros and amour must disappear from one's life.

How often I was hearing that in my counseling sessions. "We don't have anything in common anymore" frequently meant that the partnership was bereft of intimacy. There was no touching, kissing or hugging, let alone lovemaking; physical expressions of love had been banished, and along with them the most elemental love emotions were stilled.

Thank goodness those attitudes are changing. "It's all in the mind" sounds trite, but it's true. Our mindset is dramatically different from that of two or three generations ago. Some, but not all, of us now know that it is both right and normal for "older people" to have intimate thoughts and to share intimate moments with their partners. And not only is it right and normal, it is essential to one's mental/emotional health.

The nineteenth century German philosopher Arthur Schopenhauer wrote once, "All truth passes through three stages. First, it is ridiculed. Second, it is violently opposed. Third, it is accepted as being self-evident."

In the matter of senior love, I'd rewrite Schopenhauer's thought. First, it is denied, that is, "seniors have
no business thinking such ideas," and then it is ridiculed
and opposed as somehow unnatural and immoral, especially if one is widowed. Part of my growing up was in a
seafarers' village; the number of black shrouded widows
haunts me still. Only within the last couple of generations has senior love become widely recognized and
more or less acceptable. It is not yet an idea that has
achieved self evidence.

❦   ❦   ❦

When I was a college student I also was a wet-
behind-the-ears part-time student minister of a small,
rural parish. In those days and in that location, an "educated" person was respected as having superior knowledge.

I didn't have much knowledge, superior or otherwise. Some of my parishioners reinforced that delusion
by asking for my help. Eventually, I earned some university degrees and had the parchments to prove how smart
I was. I had received a classic education in theology and
philosophy and an extensive education, including
internships, in sociology and psychology. I was the
(then) modern, educated, world-class know-it-all.

One thing I did recognize quickly, however—
although only reluctantly did I allow that knowledge to
surface—was that my formal education was only a
beginning. Not until I left the ivory tower classroom and
the controlled environments of my internships did the
word "commencement" have any meaning. On the day

I received my graduate degree, I didn't realize my true education was about to begin.

With my wife and year-old daughter, I left the university, my psychology internships, and my part-time parish ministry to become the full-time minister of a suburban church. My predecessor had been widely known and respected for his counseling services. I was hired with the assumption that I would continue those services, which reached far beyond the traditional, parochial role of "pastoral counseling." Fortunately, I had the education and the training for support.

In those days few states oversaw counselors. One could claim to be a counselor and "have a practice," so to speak. I more or less inherited one, and because my church office was on a main street, I was often visited by people I did not know who sought all kinds of assistance. Additionally, in the days before social service agencies were widely available, I took referrals from what was then called the city's "welfare department," which just happened to be staffed by members of my new church.

To be a competent and constructive counselor in what then was an unregulated profession and to be regarded with respect meant, at the least, doing no harm. I considered my counseling relationship with everyone very carefully. I would decide if I could help a person. If I decided I could not, I cultivated the resources and the professionals who could, including getting financial assistance for those unable to pay for psychiatric services.

Most people who seek or are referred to counseling have temporarily lost their way. They doubt their ability to handle the future because, in most instances, they aren't able to deal with the present. They are afraid or confused or feel inadequate. Answers elude them, often because they are asking the wrong questions. Additionally, most believe they are alone and that no one has ever experienced their particular problem.

For the counselor, it's important to recognize both the individual and the individuality of his or her dilemma. Whatever it is, for that person it is unique. Chances are the counselor is the first person with whom that person's concerns have been shared fully.

The counselor must recognize that "experiencing a life problem," to coin a phrase, does not suggest one has a psychological or personality disorder. On the other hand, a competent counselor will recognize the signs of such disorders and make appropriate recommendations for that person's help.

I want to make a serious point at this juncture. After I left my ministries, which I'll mention again in a moment, I moved to a middle-class neighborhood, and once it became known what I did, I had numerous requests, usually from mothers, to "test my child." "I know you have tests for [aptitude, personality, I.Q., take your pick] and it would so help our child if we could know [whatever]." That was the general gist of many requests.

I refused all such requests as politely as I could. There were competent psychologists and psychiatrists within minutes of the neighborhood, some of whom had been my friends for years. I didn't have a high regard for the local school counselors I knew, and if a parent made a particularly compelling request for help, I made referrals, often to either Harvard or Tufts' schools of education where complete assessments could be made.

But my chief reasons for refusal were two. First, I knew the parents only wanted good reports so they could say that "Suzie scored high on her personality (or whatever) test." Second, if counseling was really needed, no neighborhood child would like to live next door to someone who knows her or his secrets. While no worthy counselor would ever reveal what was said (over the years my wife must have had a million unanswered, unspoken questions), the client, especially a minor child, just naturally harbors the fear of being revealed.

I had one other ministry, another suburban church. That church had many elderly members, as most religious bodies do. It also had scores of adolescents and teenagers, many of whom needed help growing up. That was in the mid-1950s, when unbridled unrest among youths was just becoming apparent: desegregation, the full impact of Viet Nam, free love, drugs, counter-culture punk rock. All hell was breaking loose; the wonderful youthful age of innocence was ending with an explosion; youths were about to experience forces and "demons" they couldn't imagine. They believed the world was confronting "The Eve of Destruction," as one of their songs said.

For a dozen years I had counseled the aged, the

middle-aged, and the young, helping people deal with every life crisis imaginable. Then my career took a turn. I became involved with counseling institutional and corporate leaders, helping them deal with themselves, thus helping them find ways to become better leaders of people as well as more productive managers. Institutional counseling is a big business now; it was a relatively new idea in the 1950s and 1960s, not only evaluating the institution or the business at hand, but working directly with the people who were making their organizations work. Today, many corporations, institutions and governmental bodies have human resource departments, complete with trained and knowledgeable psychologists.

I traveled constantly, often for several months at a time, in North America and in Europe. After one long trip, my young son greeted me with the question, "Are you my other grandfather?" He did not know who I was!

Then and there I decided I had to make a serious career adjustment. I had invested another eleven years in dealing with other people's lives and hadn't seen what was happening in the lives of those closest to me. My wife and I had long discussions about the possibility of unemployment. We agreed to "think about it," and we did. I had a year's worth of commitments, and I had to honor those. Then, the next spring, we decided "No more." It was time for me to be close to home, time to be a father to children who needed one. Over the telephone we agreed: complete the work in process, formally withdraw from consideration for other jobs, take a vacation, and find a new job. I did all the things necessary for my final clients—and closed down my affairs on July 31 that year.

In September I became a secondary school teacher, a psychological tester, and once again, a youth counselor. The first two years I also worked part-time as a counselor of convicts sentenced to the state prison drug addiction center.

In my new school position, I had the opportunity to work with the teachers and guidance counselors into whose hands parents gave their children. The idea that trained school counselors could be of service to parents was not new, but it was not widely accepted at the time, nor was the idea that children in need often meant a family in need. Even the poorer school districts began hiring psychologists who worked with the whole family.

For a dozen years that idea worked, caught on elsewhere—and in many places stopped suddenly. Family counseling was vigorously questioned by taxpayers; school committees began to see potential legal liability problems; budgets were cut; teacher training programs were curtailed. Psychological services, along with art and music, were expendable because government mandated programs, federal and state, were demanding more than cities and towns could afford. Intensive counseling became a luxury. After twelve years, I retired from my school.

For fifty years I have been counseling people; sometimes I've known what I was doing; occasionally I have helped. Once, my wife and I were in a restaurant, and I recognized the husband and father of a young family there. He had been one of my students, an abused child from a severely dysfunctional family. He came to our table. Yes, I remembered him, and yes, it had been years ago. Could he introduce his wife and children? I was pleased to meet them and to know the wonderful family he had. Nothing was said about his many sessions with me. After some pleasant small talk, the family returned to their table.

As we were leaving the restaurant, one of the small children came and asked if she could kiss me. I was taken aback. "My father says you saved his life and made our family possible." In the car, I had a hard time explaining to my wife the tears that streaked my cheeks. That chance meeting suddenly made a lot of things worthwhile. I had made a difference—at least once.

Oh, I made many mistakes, especially in my own life. I remember one of my children asking me, if I lived my life over, would I make the same mistakes? No, I said, I wouldn't make the same mistakes; I'd make different ones.

I didn't, but I wanted to add that we can learn from our mistakes. I think my daughter knew that anyway. Certainly she does now. And making mistakes often comes from being willing to risk failure and disappointment when we try new things and dare new adventures.

Whether my age and being widowed, my counseling experiences and the fact that I have been a second chance participant in seeking a new love are enough to help you, only you can decide.

It is said often by way of criticism that psychology (counseling) is just applying common sense, the suggestion being that anyone emotionally screwed up or twisted or whose way is lost only has to sit down with himself or herself and figure out the way. Would that it were that easy! It's not that we don't want to be mentally and emotionally healthy, it's that, as with physical problems, we may need assistance. If we have physical aches and pains, we go to a medical professional for help. So with emotional pain; sometimes we need someone to help ease our ego suffering or point us toward a better way of dealing with guilt or doubt or steer us toward a more healthy outlook about ourselves and the world in which we live.

Only guardedly do I ever just flat out offer direct advice. Usually I don't tell people what to do, but I help them find their own answers or direction.

Offering advice without helping the individual share in the discovery of self wisdom is gratuitous at best, and free advice generally is worthless, especially in a counseling situation in which one of the goals is for the individual to gain self-understanding and to move on from there. Not only that, advice given is easily ignored because the counselor has made decisions not rightfully his or hers to make.

In the matter of seniors in love, I do offer some suggestions. Whether you act upon them is your choice. And I will offer this one bit of up front advice: if there is a chance you can find love and happiness with someone new, risk it. You may fail. Yet, if you don't try, you'll

never know what might have been, and that may be
your greatest life failure.

❦　❦　❦

Thought is what defines the human, acknowledging
that to a degree many creatures may have thoughts. We
apprehend or create out of nothing certain ideas, and
then we respond to those ideas. As with the chicken and
the egg, we can argue endlessly about which came first,
awareness of something or our thinking about that
something.

Love is a thought. Like all thoughts, it takes up no
space. One might be in a closed room with a single
thought or with a hundred thoughts, and there would
be space for more. If we could gather all the thoughts
from throughout history, they would take up no physical
space.

Thoughts are—or they are not, which is different
from having positive and negative thoughts. Love is a
positive thought; hate also is a thought, leading a whole
lexicon of other negative thoughts.

Physically, we are creatures of the universe; literally,
our bodies contain cosmic stardust and elements of the
seas and of the earth, particles that create our bodies. But
all of that is not what comprises a human being.

We became human with thought. Aware of our
existence, undoubtedly first with our self-existence, we
sought the meaning of what we were and what our
world was. The first time we asked a question, we began
the unconscious struggle to achieve our humanity.

Our vocabularies, Bantu, Chinese, Russian, Greek,

English, and a myriad more mother tongues, are filled with thoughts, not one of which takes up any room in our minds, the idea of "mind" itself being another of those thoughts, along with "soul," "spirit," "purpose," "being," and countless other ideas that get into our heads.

We know many of humanity's ideas have been false answers and destructive dead ends based on a single misguided thought or a combination of such thoughts. We have yet to achieve our richest humanity. Contemporary events make one wonder if we will achieve it—which is different from if we can.

Of the hundreds of thousands of years of human existence, back to our primal beginnings, with all of humanity's failures, there has been present a sense of "something" that needs to be worked out and shared.

Paleontologists and anthropologists presently working in a cave at Bau l'Aubesier in the Vaucluse region of France have, with their discovery of a Neanderthal male jawbone and other fossil evidence of a domestic society, pushed what is called "human behavior" back 200,000 years. Perhaps Neanderthal mammoth hunters were not the savage ancestors we have thought them to be. Someone took care of a toothless old hunter. Could it have been someone who loved him?

We wonder when love began, long before our human ancestors discovered it. Swans and numerous other birds and a very few animals mate for life and are regarded favorably for their fidelity. Is that love? With the human animal, could our earliest ancestors have created families and villages and tribes without love? We know love was present in joyful measure as far back as we can trace history. When we experience love, we're not experiencing anything new to humankind; we are experiencing an old emotion anew.

Some call love the basic truth of the universe. It is sometimes called "The Way." It is what every woman knows, what every man knows, what every artist, whether painter, playwright, or musician, knows, what every philosopher knows. Within us is a single thought waiting to be released.

And that thought is love.

By itself that thought is incomplete, is nothing until it is shared, until the skillful, gentle touch of spirit as well as hands give and receive, expanding physical life into shared thought.

When one loves, then today is better than yesterday and tomorrow is a heavenly day in which spirits and bodies are joined; life surges toward wholeness, continuing toward completeness. Not completion, for that would be the end of life. When one is in love and is loved, then one senses that someone is helping to make life more meaningful and more worthwhile.

Love as a thought has so many different levels it's necessary to define just what thought we mean. If we were dealing with international and ethnic concerns, love would be such thoughts as agape, brotherly love, charity, grace, and reverence for life. Were we considering social behavior, love would be all of the above plus accord, amity, appreciation, benefiting from, caring for, harmony, rapport, sympathy. All of these thoughts are vital to what we call "our humanity." In this book, however, we are about to deal with a thought much more personal: love as eros, amour, passion, intimacy, romance.

Each facet of the love thought is relevant and meaningful, but in the erotic, passionate, intimate relationship of two people, it is much more—and on a different level. It is animal and spiritual. At its best, love not only unites two minds and bodies, it joins two souls in a shared search for their individual and mutual fulfillment.

Our focus here is on finding and holding a new love and lover after you have been separated from your former loved one because of death or divorce or estrangement. The thought of love remains; what you do with that thought may determine the rest of your life.

❦ ❦ ❦

There's knowledge and there's wisdom. Wisdom is using knowledge wisely and creatively. You know that, but stating the obvious allows me to say a word about intuition. By intuition I don't mean knowing what will happen next or knowing who you will meet before you do or sensing a disaster before it happens. By intuition I mean a kind of psychic awareness of who and what you are and what your world is. There's a lot of talk these days about "psychic energy," calling intuition our "sixth sense," claiming that intuition can led to telepathy, clairvoyance, powers of prophesy. I am not a believer.

But I do believe that our knowledge, wisdom, and life experiences can guide us. Love often is the result of an intuitive reaction to someone. There is no rational rhyme or reason; we just fall in love.

Nothing is wrong with that. But our intuition might tell us whether the love we have is good for us or bad. Will I be uplifted or will I be hurt? Can we bridge our differences or will they divide us? Is this love forever or is it a six-month escapade? Am I the only one or just one of several? Intuition doesn't ask the questions, wisdom does, but intuition might lead you to the answers.

❦   ❦   ❦

Having stated a conflict, let me conclude this chapter with another, more positive thought. In love there is spirituality. The love relationship is a journey, not a destination; a work in progress, not a work completed; fulfilling, not total fulfillment; healing, not a final cure; a search for wholeness, not ultimate achievement. Love is continual learning and sharing, a hand-in-hand partnership in which two people are joined mentally and emotionally—and physically—in reaching for their heaven.

In their union they do not become one organism; they are two unique individuals who have created a deep, mutual partnership, each believing life's journey is best taken with the other. Along the way they increase their trust of and respect for their partner, they release their hurts and are comforted, they dream great dreams and are empowered to pursue them. They raise partnership to a level that allows each and both to reach for the moon and the stars. In their way, lovers rise above the mundane and grime and create an emotional environment above the ordinary.

A Second Chance

You ask yourself, is it natural for someone, a member of "the senior generation," to fall in love? Yes, it is. It's as natural as falling off a log, and maybe just as dangerous. We'll get to the risks in due time. Age has nothing to do with love or love with age. The poet and playwright William Butler Yeats was in his seventies when he wrote:

> An aged man is but a paltry thing,
> A tattered coat upon a stick, unless
> Soul clap its hands and sing, and
> louder sing....
> —From *Sailing to Byzantium*

By definition *unless* means "if the condition changes." And what would change that old, paltry human? Why, one's inner soul clapping its hands and singing for love, for life yet to be lived, for accomplishments yet to be achieved, for living hand in hand with someone and with that person joining hands and singing loudly.

Of course, there are those who whimper Elizabeth Akers Allen's plea: "Backward, turn backward, O Time, in your flight," and wish for some kind of biological Jules Verne time machine, but that isn't going to happen. We are what our years make us—seniors.

The key to unlocking beauty and light in our senior years, Yeats' "soul," if you will, is what we make of the years left, not what we wish for and cannot recapture from the past. Age, as has been said innumerable times, is often a matter of the mind and not the mere accumulation of years. Just as aging in and of itself doesn't make us any wiser, although it should, aging does not preclude our ability to give and receive love in the most intimate sense.

Whether you should allow yourself the joy of loving (again) depends on whether you want to. And if you want to, whether you are willing to work at it and—a sobering thought—whether you're willing to risk your ego.

Some seniors view the act of loving and being loved with trepidation if not outright fear and would agree with Albert Einstein, "I live in that solitude which is painful in youth, but delicious in the years of maturity," not realizing that Einstein separated from both his wives because, he said, a wife was a poor second to his love of physics (and, he admitted, his later obsession with Marilyn Monroe).

Especially once he arrived in America, Einstein said and wrote many wonderful and insightful lines, but his solitude was an abnormal defense against any close personal relationship. Solitude which is more than temporary is an escape; Einstein to the contrary, we live best and richest when we live with and for someone we love.

❦   ❦   ❦

The need to love and to be loved has nothing to do with age—and here I'm speaking of romantic love, that love which brings two hearts, two minds, two bodies together in union. That's what this book is about: older people finding and holding someone to love and being loved by that someone; in other words, two people creating a second —or perhaps a first—life partnership.

I use the designation *partner* rather than *companion* because this book is about building a lasting and meaningful relationship, amour, if you like that word, and romance. A mere companion, thus a companionship, lacks the intensity of a romantic relationship. Partner, thus a partnership, implies a relationship between equals. Also, companion often has the connotation of someone serving another while partner carries within its meaning mutual sharing, a concept about which I devote an entire chapter.

This book is about senior love and the steps necessary to find and hold a loving partner. The book is divided into chapters using lines from my poem "The Steps of Love" as chapter headings. The poem is printed in whole at the end of the book.

❦ ❦ ❦

"The mind is always the dupe of the heart," reads François Duc de La Rochefoucauld's maxim number 102. Emily Dickinson carried the thought further: "The Mind lives on the Heart / Like any Parasite—."

Dupe. Parasite. Loaded words, but true, and therein the seniors' (and everyone's, for that matter) situation: love is an emotion seldom surrendering itself to intellectual analysis and understanding. Love is one of those emotional junctions where mind and body meet; the thought of loving someone causes changes in the biochemistry of your body. The thought in your mind becomes a visceral, not a brainy thing, an emotion felt in your body, the heart being of the viscera, and as we know well, the heart can and does control the head.

We refer often to the "foolish heart," acknowledging that the heart leads us, not the brain. Sometimes the heart does dupe the mind—as when in love. Whether the mind lives entirely off the heart is doubtful, although in loving it does seem so.

When it comes to seniors, Rochefoucauld has another maxim, number 423: "Few people know how to be old." Our mothers said it differently, "Act your age." That might have been appropriate when we were ten; it's far more profound when we are seventy.

I'm not sure I know how to act my age, how to act at being old. My body tells me I have aged, and the mirror reflects what my body tells me. My mind rebels against any thought insinuating that somehow, because I have accumulated years, my mind is less nimble or less active or less acute. I am young because my mind and heart have stayed young.

My heart knows nothing of age. In that, the heart may dupe the mind, in which case it's a wonderful bit of "That Old Black Magic has me in its spell" kind of stuff, a condition in which many seniors find themselves.

Our senior generation is learning how to be old and how to act its age: unconventionally, by letting the eternal youthfulness of our hearts rule over what used to be called "common sense" and "propriety" and, yes, "acting one's age."

When we put age (being older) and love together, we

begin to understand François and Emily. No matter our age, the heart rules the mind; our brains and bodies feed off the emotions of our hearts. In love, we are perpetually young.

I shout bravo! Who has the right to tell you cannot be romantic, cannot date, cannot love? Not only do you have the right to seek love and to give love, this book will guide you through the steps of love, from the first time you are aware of a special someone to when you may be singing in praise of a union of loving partners.

❦ ❦ ❦

We seniors are pre-Beatles, pre-LPs, pre-birth control pills, pre-space shuttles, pre-TV. We are just about pre-everything, before polio vaccines, before commercial jetliners, before heart/lung/kidney transplants. We are the children of the Great Depression and World War II. We are senior citizens; some of us are senior-seniors, those who remember Prohibition and the three presidents (Harding, Coolidge, Hoover) before Roosevelt (the FDR version).

We are in our sixties, seventies, and eighties; we were born in the 1920s, '30s and '40s. By our numbers, we create some social problems. There are a lot of us living far longer than actuaries figured we would. As a group, we are hale and hearty and more active than any generation before us. We not only travel, we hike and canoe, play golf and softball in unprecedented numbers, and we buy homes for our next hundred years.

We are life participants, not spectators. We have not taken growing old or aging lying down. If anything, we grab hold of life and shake it for all it's worth. And we seem to be having a ball, throwing off inhibitions and freeing ourselves from social restraints and conventions, freeing ourselves from concerns about taste and propriety and impressing our peers, not caring what the neighbors or our children say until—following the death of or separation from a mate—we forge or create new intimate relationships.

For all the singing and talking our children and grandchildren do about falling in love, younger generations draw the line when it's their parents and grandparents and great grandparents who are doing the loving. It's just not done, they say, as if rekindling the romantic spark somehow is immoral and sinful—unless it leads to marriage, in which case that's okay because the old folks are chaste and beyond knowing the pleasures of the flesh.

Our children and grandchildren think we don't know, to use Mark Twain's thought, the difference between lightning and a lightning bug. If only they knew! Or perhaps they know and don't want to face up to the fact that mom or dad, grandma or grandpa not only *can* do it but *want* to do it and *will* do it if and when the right partner comes along. The truth is, seniors fall in love and express their love in exactly the same way youngsters do.

I always wonder just what will happen when adult children are brought into a new relationship. The partners provide an opportunity for the children to meet one another and to evaluate the potential new member of the family. Then, too often, that member is evaluated along with his or her children, and judgments are made.

Many a "match made in heaven" has gone down the drain after such meetings. "He isn't up to our standards." "How could you be happy with her?" "He's just after your money." "You're too good for her." "His children are kluks." And so on.

"Checking out" is natural; so is wanting to protect one's mother or father, but children ought to remember that the relationship got this far because of some kind of emotional chemistry and emotional reaction between the two parents. The children's role is to accept that fact and to help good things happen, not to cut up or put down their parent's potential life partner.

So the other's children are idiots; they may have the same opinion of their counterparts. So the new important person in a parent's life is not a Greek god or goddess. They're hard to find anywhere.

What gets lost in the checking-out process in which children engage are the two parents and their happiness, present and future.

It's not unknown that children are jealous. They're losing their parent to a stranger; they're losing their special place in the parent's universe; they're being replaced! They aren't, of course, but try telling that to the possessive child who wants no competition.

❧ ❧ ❧

Two things this book is not. Caveat emptor. First, this is not a sex guide, a "how-to-do-it" manual for the elderly. In every bookstore there are shelves full of guides for those who need help (or a refresher course for those unsure of themselves) if "doin' what comes nacherly" doesn't happen. The fact of sexual activity is recognized in this book, but mostly that recognition deals with mutually achieved attitudes about sexual events; sexual techniques are absent.

Second, this book is not a guide for dealing with the loss of a loved partner either by death or separation (that is, divorce). We, the author included, are widowed or separated. In no way are the two the same; only the situation in which we find ourselves is common: we are without love and loving partners. And we think we have found or might find someone who might become that loved and loving partner.

❦ ❦ ❦

Ago, perhaps over a long period of time, we had a love. I don't know your particular circumstance, whether your love was a brief affair, a half century of bliss, or one that turned into a life-long bitter sentence you served because you took your marriage vows seriously, whether your separation loss was a crushing blow or a decree of freedom from abuse and debasement.

Whatever, you are now a free woman or a free man. The author makes the assumption you have come to terms with your mate's death or separation. If you haven't, you have no business thinking about new, intimate relationships. You carry too much negative baggage to achieve a relationship that is meaningful, stable, and lasting.

If you are looking for one-night stands, choose

carefully. You can buy sex, make all kinds of erotic connections; you can even buy a companion, but by definition you cannot buy a partner. Just as surely, you cannot buy affection and respect. Certainly, you cannot buy love. I don't know where I first heard the line "throwing one's body before the heart." It provides a caution; in some instances never is the heart involved. I hope you have set your sights higher; whoever you meet worthy of your attention will have set his or her sights high.

Seniors in Love is about the possible next step after you have adjusted to your loss, that is, seeking, finding and keeping someone to love and be loved by, a new special friend, a life partner, a lover, a mate in ways that are mutually morally and spiritually healthy and fulfilling—and lasting. And that is far more profound than casual sex.

So, you are in the September of your life.

And you are single.

Things happen.

Affections happen.

Love happens.

❦ ❦ ❦

This is your reality, the fact that love is not limited by age and that older people can be and are as passionate, loving and seeking as any teenager. And perhaps because of age and experiences, should you find someone to love, you can and will be more loving, more caring, more attuned to that person.

And therein lies one of the senior generation's

mysteries (at least to those not yet seniors): how, and maybe why, do seniors fall in love and practice intimacy? There should be no mystery about it.

Most seniors were raised in the mid-twentieth century, but much like children of the Victorian Age. Love, let alone sex, never was a topic of conversation among adults when children were present. I doubt that it was even when we were not present. We got our education behind the barn or wherever groups of girls or groups of boys gathered to share their ignorance. We are an original "don't ask, don't tell" generation. I never asked; I had little to tell. If my peers knew twice what I knew about sex and male-female relationships, they proved only our individual and collective ignorance. It's as the former *Tonight* show host, Johnny Carson, said: "I was so naive as a kid I used to sneak behind the barn and do nothing."

We remain ignorant to this day, not about the sexual "how to do it" part; we're inept when it comes to speaking loving words, expressing love, communicating love thoughts. And often we are inept in receiving and responding to love. We don't always know how to behave or know what to say. Not responding with warmth makes us appear cold. Meaningful demonstrations of affection, when they are present, make us uncomfortable. The rigid morality of an earlier age, the veil of silence and propriety still hangS over us. That and guilt. It's time to free ourselves from both.

❦   ❦   ❦

Some of the thoughts contained in this book have been said by seniors. I have recollected, distilled and incorporated individual senior's ideas and experiences, adding them to my own experiences both personal and as a counselor. This is not a psychological or sociological report of a study of seniors' activities and feelings. The only thing I am reporting is my interpretation of a life experience, seniors who fall in love and the risks and joys, the fulfillment and disappointments that may be present and how we might get from the first step, discovering someone, to the last step, the potential union, whether formalized or not, of two people who love each other.

When I started to write this book, I wrote some paragraphs in the third person. They were sterile and dishonest. This is not a third person novel in which the author, like a god, looks down to report what's happening among earth's creatures. When a novel is written in the third person, the storyteller remains apart from the story, tells someone else's story. I'm not writing about fictional characters; I'm writing about myself and you and people I know or have known and about our second chance for love and happiness and about the steps, as I see them, we have to take to reach beyond pleasure to happiness.

For a senior, being in love following separation from a former loved one is traveling into the unknown territory of a foreign country; one leaves behind the familiar. One has never been here before, not like this. Now one is not talking about the old days; one is speaking of a new day—not yesterday, but today and tomorrow.

❦ ❦ ❦

In these early pages, there are some essential chores to be done. I want to address three issues raised by those mental health professionals who read drafts of this book.

First, one reader insisted I make it clear that finding someone to love, a second chance, is not a license to hunt. Chasing, running down or after, or hounding a might-be partner (lover, mate) inevitably, that reader said, leads to disaster. I've tried to make that clear in later chapters. Finding someone to love happens; sustained love seldom happens when one goes "hunting." *How to Marry a Millionaire* is great comedy, but as even the movie suggested, the spark of love does not come from devious plots and ploys and repeated chases; love happens because two people create a single fire that burns in both hearts. We hope, using Dante's words, that "A great flame follows a little spark." The idea of hunting bothered another psychologist, too. She wrote in the margin, "If you look, you will never find it (love). It's when you stop looking that it happens (or bites you in the butt)."

The second issue was raised by a note a hundred pages into an early draft of the book, "Have you thought about homosexual relationships?" It's a proper question.

Although my sexual orientation is "straight," or heterosexual, I had given thought to homosexual love and lovers. Perhaps, to be fair, each chapter should have paragraphs addressed specifically to same sex relationships. I haven't done that, not because of disrespect or prejudice but because I think in terms of male-female relationships. To me, a person's sexual orientation is not an issue. I present my thoughts based on my orientation, selecting from my experience and from my interpretation of others' experiences. That's the author's bias and privilege.

Moreover, what is laid out here seems to me to apply regardless of one's sexual orientation. Discovering someone to love, reaching out to that someone, loving that someone and creating a partnership are steps of love that apply whether you hope to establish a lasting relationship with someone of the same sex or the opposite sex. Giving love is offering yourself to another; receiving love is being offered a self in return. When mutual love results in a lasting partnership, your and your lover's world is right and secure.

I do raise two storm warnings, however. The first warning concerns bisexuality. If either you or your intended partner is bisexual, that is, if one or the other is physically attracted to people of both sexes, in such instances seldom does a solid partnership result. I'm inclined to say never. I don't know any statistics to differentiate between seldom and never, but I do know that when even one partner is bisexual, a failed relationship is inevitable because that partner will seek out other physical relationships, gay or lesbian. Additionally, bisexual individuals, by their own testimony, seldom seem able to maintain a lasting love relationship and often claim they can be in love with two or several other persons of both genders at the same time. If that is true, it reduces love to the level of lust, not a very solid foundation upon which to build a partnership of love.

Thus the second warning, which has to do with polyamory, the practice, if that is the proper word, of being romantically in love with two or several people (sometimes of both genders) at the same time and of expressing that love in the most intimate ways possible. Interest in polyamory is increasing, not all of it healthy, some of it simply having to do with multiple sex partners, some of it having to do with one's inability to make a commitment to a relationship, some of it having to do with the effort to discover one's sexuality. It's not within the scope of this book, but many of the reasons for embracing polyamory suggest an individual need for help in sorting out a lot of issues. As with bisexuality (many practitioners of polyamory are bisexual), the foundation for a stable one-with-one relationship is not present.

The third issue is a reader's two-pronged reaction, questioning the "steps of love." First, it was suggested that the way I (artificially?) divided the book into chapters is not the way to achieve and practice love. Second, that reader suggested that everyone knows what love is and how to practice it anyway.

In one way I agree with the first part of that criticism. In discovering someone, reaching out to that someone, making plans with that someone, all kinds of things are going on in the mind and heart of a person at the same time. My rationale in dividing the whole love affair into segments or steps is that the whole cannot be taken in or accomplished all at once; it would be like viewing the forest without ever seeing the trees, or if you don't like that metaphor, it would be like constructing a building before you know what's going into it.

Not all seniors need to be reminded of what goes into a loving relationship. We think we know, having been there, done that. But the truth is, we don't always know, or we have forgotten, that while loving someone is easy, the fact of loving is a lifetime of proving and maintaining the loving partnership.

Okay, you know what love is, and you know how to make love. Let this book remind you of the foundation upon which love is built; let it remind you that love is achieved selflessly; let it remind you that love is constructed day be day, loving act by loving act. You may not learn anything new; you may learn how to use your knowledge creatively.

❦ ❦ ❦

While from the beginning I have focused this book on discovering and creating a new love relationship, here I want to remind ourselves that everything said can and does apply to existing relationships which have not been ended but which are on the edge of disunion.

Over a period of time, I worked with a man of great creative talent. When he first came to me, he was in the process of throwing away not only his genius but his wife and children. He became a drunk, then a classic alcoholic; his "new" friends were talented drunks, and what pleasure they couldn't find in drink, some found with willing women. My man was honored by his professional peers and jeered at and shunned by his neighbors.

He didn't care; he didn't even know what he was doing. He lost his job; his children moved away, denying him any contact. He might have lost his house had his wife not been employed.

Our relationship lasted for six years, on and off. He needed me because I understood his problem; he didn't need me because I knew him too well. From time to time I'd manage to get him into a treatment center and under the care of a psychiatrist. He always discharged himself after a few days or a couple of weeks.

Finally he told me, "Leave me the hell alone."

With him, I had failed. Fifteen years later, I received a note from his wife—"Burt" wanted to see me.

Burt had been institutionalized for years; his drinking had ended; he still lived with his wife in what at best could be described as an armed truce. The question he posed was simple: could I help them resurrect their marriage?

For them to do that seemed almost impossible. First, I lived hours away. We trust you, they said. I'll find someone. You know us better than anyone. It will be hard work. We are committed to making it work.

Some of what is written here is the proof of their dedication to a marriage long thought dissolved. They did recreate their sense of love and unity; they shared in the reconstruction of their lives. They had wasted almost a half century, yet in their old age, until their deaths, the last twelve years were priceless. Worth the defeats and struggles? They would tell you yes.

❦ ❦ ❦

The very idea of loving someone and being loved by someone makes us feel good. If we are lucky enough to discover someone, then we must be brave enough to seek out that someone, and if he or she responds positively to our approach, we must be wise enough to build emotional bridges of love, respect and partnership.

And if we discover someone, it is not only our heart that is aflame and beating with loving rhythms; we must set his or her heart on fire and then work hard to synchronize the two beating, blazing hearts.

Love

Love, the sublime spirit,
drives our lives: one's heart
exchanged with another,
doubts and fears to outwit.

Before we even discover someone who might ignite our heart, before we give thought to whether we want to love someone again, before we wonder if someone might love us, let's consider what love is, what we're talking about—just in case the thought ever arises.

Love is an idea.
It gets in our heads.

"Here is someone who gives me beauty, who takes my breath away, who nurtures my ego and enlarges it. I want to—I must—include that special person in my life. Love is the single-minded thought from deep within myself that separated from that person I am incomplete."

Have you ever said that? Are you thinking it now?

We reach down into ourselves, almost without realizing it, and draw upon the idea. The idea illuminates our lives. No matter what, we are more aware of self. Our self needs an other—and surprisingly, allowing that thought into our lives expands our self-awareness.

Where does the idea come from? We don't know. Some say it is not "real." But when love happens, to us it is real; it becomes our reality.

These truths we know: loving builds our ability to love; loving gives us the courage to love; being loved has the power to strengthen and will strengthen our self-image.

We love ourselves first. Self-preservation is both natural and necessary. Assured through struggle, it is not enough. Wholeness is seldom achieved alone. We know that. Wholeness comes when there is someone to hold and to be held by, someone for whom to care and who cares about us, someone with whom to share and who shares.

Pairing is an elemental fact of life, the essential animal fact, if you will, but for the human it is more sublime than the physically erotic. We pair together in love, and certainly that includes physical passion, but having said that, love is more than, deeper than, and beyond the physical.

Our loved one is seen not "as is," but is seen as the indispensable single other ego-self that impacts upon and recreates our lives. The *I* is not replaced; it is expanded into *we*. Life is not lived for *me*; life is lived for *us*. This is *our* world and *our* time.

Recently, I watched a man present an emotionally charged, difficult, important, and controversial point of view to a skeptical audience. Finished, he sat down next to his wife. As he did, she reached out and patted his arm and then held it.

I was moved by the gesture. To me she was saying, "You did your best, even if people didn't like it. I love you. I stand by you."

Of course, she could have been saying just the opposite, that is, "Nice try, Loser"—but I don't think so. Some who witnessed her behavior had a contrary reaction. To them the touch was mawkish and soupy and unsophisticated. I recall Ben Jonson's line popping into my head: "Preserving the sweetness of proportion and expressing itself beyond expression." I found the wife's touch just right, and had I been that man, the touch would have been sublime. It said more than any word; it was an affirmation of love and togetherness.

Love is bold, daring and demanding, and you may be thinking about it again.

We know what love is, or at least we think we do, but we have a hard time defining it. When love comes to us, we try to describe it, what it does to us, how it makes us feel. We use metaphors and similes, and when love is good, we seek to capture its essence so we can relay to the one we love the deep, irrepressible feelings we have. It's an effort not always successful, because when we are in love it's sometimes impossible to voice the profound emotional condition in which we have become enwrapped.

Love is the delicate smell of the earth after a summer rain ... the scorching sun's blaze bursting through dark clouds ... as tender as a mother's

touch...as raucous as a New Orleans jazz band at
Mardi Gras.

Love is ... supporting arms in moments of
endeavor, loving arms in moments of passion,
uplifting arms in moments of need, welcoming
arms forever...is putting one's heart into another's
hand, knowing it is safe from all harm....

These words I wrote once, maybe not very much different from words you have thought or used. Trying to
express love, we become poets and musicians and artists,
most of us not very good but each attempting to speak
or sing or show the idea that might join us together with
the one we love.

Poet Margaret Atwood ends her poem "We are
Hard" with the question, "If I love you / is that a fact or
a weapon?"

When I speak about seniors in love, I mean romantic
love, an affair of the heart that goes beyond agape or
charity, beyond friendship even. I'm speaking about passionate affection for, adoring, being enamored of, losing
one's heart to, luxuriating in someone. Such feelings are
much different and far more intense than simply being
fond of, feeling tenderness toward, or having warm feeling for a person.

The word *romance* (like the word *cleave*) has two
meanings that are diametrically opposed to each other.
As a verb, one connotation is of a love story—a tale of
chivalry; the other is as an extravagant story that has no
basis in fact. As a verb, *romance* can mean "to carry on a

love affair with," or it can mean "to exaggerate, to invent details or incidents, or to flatter." Seniors seeking love need to understand that when I say love, I mean romance, as in passion, adoration, how a certain someone lights you up from within.

Nevertheless, when love is expressed, the hearer may suspect a lack of truth, that in fact the love spoken may be a complete invention or a major exaggeration, and thus it may be an emotional weapon of abuse, as Atwood suggests. In the musical *Finian's Rainbow,* the mischievous leprechaun who is magically made human sings, "When I'm not near the girl I love, I love the girl I'm near." That's a common human sentiment. Few, male or female, would deny having had that feeling. Attractive people are everywhere, and it's natural to respond to attractive people.

That does not mean we will fall in love with every attractive person we encounter. If we do, something is wrong with our concept of love, reducing it to sexual attraction, the leprechaun's "if they've got a bosom, I woes 'em" mentality, a basic fabrication or a lustful invention, as with Kathleen Winsor's fictional (Forever) Amber or the real Casanova, both promiscuous lovers who used others to satisfy only their own sexual needs. That kind of "love" is a cruel weapon of abuse and brings misfortune and disaster.

❧ ❧ ❧

There are hundreds of definitions of love, perhaps millions. It's likely every individual in love or who thinks he or she is in love will have a personal definition.

Good! One should develop the words that give expression to what one feels.

For seniors, those words are tempered by time. We loved once. When we think about loving again, we cannot help but evaluate our former love affair(s), what we did right and what we did wrong, what was creative and what was destructive. At this point there is no useful purpose delving into the past—except to tell ourselves that whatever mistakes we made we will try not to make again.

Another aspect of time is that we are not the same person we once were, physically or emotionally. Physically, our tummies may protrude, our chests sag, our veins show, our thighs may be thicker; our muscles may hang looser, our hair may be thinner and grayer, our feet flatter, our skin less taut. We have aged. That's life's fact. I say now, if we have aging in perspective, if and when we love someone, such physical facts become irrelevant.

The emotional changes are not irrelevant. No matter how good or bad our earlier love affair was, we must carry from it good intentions. Perhaps we did not share enough, were not attentive enough, were not romantic enough. Perhaps we took the other for granted or expected too much or failed to encourage enough.

Whatever love is to you, it must include the commitment to make your partner happier, fuller, more courageous and daring, giving that partner no reason to regret having fallen in love with you.

Long before someone appears on your radar screen, long before you ask whether you can ever love again, long before you wonder if you have "the right stuff," you are doomed to failure if you do not understand and appreciate the nature of the love you might give and the nature of the love you might seek.

If love is a weapon or a tool to satisfy your loneliness or build your ego or enhance your sense of wellness, you're headed for failure, because when you are in love, you are not the important partner. The other partner is.

Think of it. You proclaim your love. What are you saying? If your love is fact, you are saying to someone, "You are the most important person in the whole world. I offer my life to you." That's what love is, giving yourself to someone else. And if love is returned, that someone gives his or her life to you.

That's an utterly awesome exchange. You made it once; now you are thinking about doing it again. If you are wise, and I assume you are, you will give more than you ever did—because you are wise enough to know that passion and adoration and all the rest are reciprocated by the measure given.

Love does not lend itself to mathematical formulas, but unless you give your entire self to your loved one, you will be shortchanged.

One thing that has always impressed me when working with couples was how often someone felt cheated (other than by infidelity) and how often that person confessed to having withheld something (expressions of love, encouragement, praise, sex) and how often that person gave love only when her or his partner did something special. Love had become a weapon, not a fact.

"I'll [whatever] as a reward.""He has to earn ——""She doesn't —— so I ——."

Often such couples don't have a clue to their difficulties. Seniors have one great advantage. It's called experience. So, if there is to be a second chance for love, let experience work for you.

A "second chance." One negative aspect of a senior's second chance begs recognition. It has no name and often is not recognized, although it is present sometimes and is debilitating. It is that somewhere in a person's past was a lover so grand that no one since can hope to measure up. That lover might have been one's former spouse, or it might have been from an earlier time or from an affair.

The love and the lover, over time, become idealized and now nothing matches and no one can live up to the former love(r). Love is all around, but the person living only in the past cannot feel it. There might even be someone to love; someone who isn't even given a chance. The condition is hinted at in the Carly Simon song, *Stuff That Dreams Are Made Of.* She asks, "What if the prince on the horse in your fairy tale is right here in disguise? / And what if the stars you've been reaching so high for are shining in his eyes?"

Yes, what if?

❦   ❦   ❦

Too many seniors mistake convenience for love. You want to live together to save expense money, have a traveling companion, have someone who will take care of the house? That's okay, but don't call that love, and when the chips are down (financial demands, ill health, or the like often provide the reality), don't be surprised when the relationship goes sour and south.

It's no accident that traditional marriage vows usually include the promise to love and to honor and to cherish "for richer, for poorer, in sickness and in health, till death do us part."

You might love and live with someone without marriage, but true love, real love, the fact of love, even without the formal vows, is explicit: through every test, love says, "I am with you; I am the everlasting arms that hold and sustain you." If you can't offer that, you never will be in love because you will be offering nothing.

And, as cruel as it may sound, you don't deserve to be loved.

❦ ❦ ❦

When we were young, the future was infinite. Seniors know how short their time really is. For many of us, the future is now; there may be second chances; there will not be too many opportunities for third and fourth and tenth chances at anything.

Many of us at this stage of our lives, if the present opportunity for love is not realized, will avoid deliberately another similar situation. We will be convinced that love is not for us or that love has passed us by. Failure at this opportunity will, in all likelihood, signal our defeat.

The lack of possible repeat opportunities does not mean to rush into a love affair; it does mean that if finding one, heaven and earth should be moved to make it as rich and as meaningful as humanly possible and as fulfilling and rewarding as you can make it!

Exclamation point! Key words: AS YOU CAN MAKE IT. *This* love affair is the one. Not the last love affair or the next one; it's the only one. If you are going to fall in love, stand naked and give everything to your love and to your loved one. The "stand naked" part I mean in a figurative sense (if it becomes literal, that's great, too), hiding nothing, withholding nothing, and by "give everything" I mean exactly that. Every fiber of your body, every brain cell, every nerve ending should go into proving your love is a fact.

"The way to a man's heart is through his stomach" might be good politics; it's bad love advice, and not just because of nutritive concerns. We live most fully and creatively when we are loved. Beyond basic food and shelter, love is the most important thing with us. To be loved is to have life given to us; to love someone is to offer that someone our whole world. It may not be enough, but it's all we have, that and an occasional red rose.

Discovering

A voice, a glance, a face
fills all your emptiness,
flows to the out most limb,
a wonder time of grace.

WOW! COOL! INSPIRING! AEAEAE AFFLATUS!

Got you on the last one, didn't I? The two words certainly are not part of our everyday speech, but in their way, they summarize the point here: a magical divine inspiration. From the Latin, *aeaeae*, magic; *afflare* has to do with the gods' breathing out, and *inspiration* means breathing in—divine stuff, and that's what we're talking about here, *aeaeae afflatus*, having our breath taken away, magical divine breathing.

We are seniors. The love that kept us warm once is no longer with us. Some, for a multitude of reasons, will remain single by choice, enjoying the freedom from and lack of responsibility for someone else; some will not want to risk another close, intimate relationship and possible loss; some cannot trust that another partner will not be abusive, physically or emotionally; potential partners may have hidden agendas masquerading as love; the sincerity of suitors is doubted.

Some will float, more or less aimlessly. The separation took something out of their lives, and whether the loss was of someone held precious or someone who drove the marriage or partnership to dissolution, the loss was a kind of emotional and spiritual defeat. One could not stop death from visiting or one could not bridge the divisions that forced the relationship to fall apart.

Some will flit from one brief relationship to another, never sure of wish or motive, becoming a kind of manipulative and manipulating whore, seeking financial if not emotional security, failing, rationalizing each encounter as "a learning experience" or "just being myself," whatever that self is—or becomes.

Some, stoic, accepting the vanities of life, will pick up the shattered pieces of their lives—and exist alone. If they have a goal, it's to survive as best they can until they die.

And some, you perhaps, will place themselves in situations where people meet and enjoy other people. It may be that you discover someone—in your church activities or at your golf club; it may be at AARP meetings or as you volunteer in hospitals or schools or recreational centers; it may be while grocery shopping and standing in the checkout line; it may be in a singles' bar; it might be while walking the dog or at the library—the occasions and locales are endless.

It happens.

You are struck by a magical divine inspiration. Someone arouses and energizes your heart and mind; someone stimulates you to a new and higher level of creativity and action; someone transforms your life by suggesting, albeit unintentionally, new vistas and new pathways for your life journey.

Not sought, not even thought, someone appears in your emotional field of vision, and suddenly the whole world changes. There is an attraction; you are drawn to that person; there is a man or a woman leading your thoughts.

The thoughts linger; you allow the thoughts to expand, and the thoughts are good.

You feel good.

What was empty begins to fill. You suck in your out-of-shape belly, redo and recolor your hair, select brighter clothing; there is a boldness to your steps, color on your face, a brightness in your eyes.

There, perhaps, is someone to fill the void, someone to fill in the missing piece of your life's puzzle, someone with whom to sing and dance and laugh and share life.

Maybe.

But—wait…. The thought is dumb. At your age, who has the right to think such thoughts? Perhaps it's even immoral to have such thoughts; old men and old women have no business thinking about dating and hugging and kissing and touching. It's sinful.

What will people say? What will the children say? Bury the thought of holding that other person in your arms.

The whole idea is ridiculous.

Stupid, even.

But the images will not go away. Bury them and they pop up stronger than ever. The body may be old; the heart and mind are young. Forever young. The years drop away. In your mind are images that cannot be shaken, fantasies you cannot dismiss, hopes you cannot kill.

There, in full view, is someone you might love, and,

may the gods and stars and fate conspire with you, someone who might love you in return.

Is the idea so far fetched? Is the potential for love given only to the young? Nonsense. Love is a matter of the heart and the heart stimulates the mind and the heart affects the body.

Is that limited to young people?

I say my mind is keener than a youngster's; my heart beats just as strongly as a youngster's. I'd like to say my body is as tuned and as athletically shaped as a young-ster's, but, as you guess, that's not true.

Can you respond to colors and shapes, sights and sounds and smells as well as any youth? Of course. You may need glasses or a hearing aid, but when stimuli reach the brain, there is no distinction of age.

A man or a woman appears and enters one's thoughts and will not leave, peacefully or otherwise. Love, or the possibility of love, is just as disconcerting as it was at eighteen, only you're not eighteen again.

So far it's all in the mind.

To take the next step, to actually approach the object of one's thoughts, is a gigantic risk of rejection, of being laughed at, of embarrassment, of ridicule.

"You're a dirty old man" or "What are you, some kind of (whatever)?" That would be bad enough. Worse would be, "Why should I be interested in you?" Worst would be, "You've got nothing but aches and pains (or have no money or need a homemaker; fill in the excuse) and want someone to take care of you."

Yes, the risk of rejection is huge.

And you are a fragile human being with a fragile psyche.

But a risk not taken is the worst kind of failure.

Go for it.

If he or she is worth it, reach out for the wonder time.

You remember Maxwell Anderson's "the days grow short, when you reach September." You're in the September of your life. There, filling your thoughts, is that someone with whom "these precious days I'll spend with you."

❦ ❦ ❦

There are no guarantees that discovering someone who fills your heart means the feeling will be reciprocated.

At this immediate moment that's not what's important.

The first step of love is that there is a person to whom you are emotionally attracted and who stirs your heart. Good for you. If nothing more, it proves you are alive and capable of having positive feelings. After your loss, that is a significant plus. After death or separation there is life. You knew that; there is life beating in the old heart.

A popular song of the 1930s was *I'll Never Smile Again*. The singer's love had withdrawn, was apart, nothing will be right "until I smile at you." Our late or former partner cannot return; for a time life stops; we wonder if we will ever smile again with the same zest and enthusiasm.

More, we wonder if there is room in our hearts for another person. Or if we should allow room for another person. And if there is and if we do, what will become of us?

All kinds of uncertainties and doubts race through our minds. That's natural. It's also natural to want to love and to be loved, and since that is natural, it is in the nature of life that in the aftermath of loss we might be drawn to another.

If you are, then go for it. Take the step. Or at least face the possibility of taking it.

Your decision. But how foolish it would be to know that there in plain view might be someone you could love and who could love you, and you did nothing about it.

When Dante's pilgrim was to pass through the gates of hell, he read the words emblazoned over the portal: "Abandon all hope ye who enter here."

Too many seniors have done just that.

Few remember that at the end of the pilgrim's journey was paradise. There are no promises, but paradise is never found by sitting on your dreams. Hope is something you want to happen, but you cannot just laze around hoping. You have to work for that something to happen because hope also is a thought you send out into the future. When you do, two things happen. First, that hope beckons you. "Come on," it says, and second, you have to go get it. "Come on, reach for me. You projected me out here, come and get me."

Now!
Grasp your opportunity.
Dare the risk.
Take the next step.

Reaching

Reach out, pursue the chance,
offer your best, and if
love be returned, embrace
your partner in love's dance.

Perhaps the idea and image of somebody has begun to live inside you. Do you keep it a secret? What do you do with the thoughts racing through your mind and unsettling your heart? If you have discovered someone whose existence in your world moves you, it is apparent you have two choices.

You can admire that person from afar, let your potential love feelings be silently in vain, in which case nothing will ever come of your attraction, or you can reach out to that person, risk rejection, and perhaps step into a new world of potential bliss. Take your pick.

If you elect not to risk rejection, you will have concluded what might have been a meaningful and wonderful life chapter.

The choice sounds easier than it is.

Remember the love song *If I Loved You,* with the line, "Longing to tell you, but afraid am I; I've let my golden chances pass me by"? You didn't want that to be your song. "Time and again I would try to say...."

So you have decided to speak up. Good for you!

We hear a lot these days about "articulation." It can mean anything from the way dual blades in a food processor are coordinated to the complicated gear box in a four-wheel vehicle, from the way our finger and toe joints work to what most of us learned in school—plain, clear speech.

When we say words of affection for the first time, our lips, teeth, palate, and vocal cords may not allow the grand articulation we have practiced. We will stumble over the words, hesitant, clumsy and doltish, ungraceful and awkward. To mix metaphors, our tongues will be all thumbs.

As Jim Croce's present rendition of the idea declares, "Every time I tried to tell you the words just came out wrong. / So I'll have to say 'I love you' in a song."

"I would try to say...." In the final analysis, it's not the song or the words that matter, not one's eloquent elocution or harmonic voice, but the honesty of what's said.

You speak of affection and attraction, perhaps withholding the "love" word, and you are not rejected entirely. Probably you will not receive an unqualified declaration of hidden love in return, not even an intimation of it, but you might receive some positive encouragement, a measure of affection, and an offer of friendship.

Now other choices are to be made: accept what was offered and be thankful for that or work all the harder to demonstrate the depth of your feelings in hope that one day that person will have great affection for you. That choice is not hard to make.

To seek that affectionate attention is worth every

effort you make. Tolstoy wrote, "The strongest of all warriors are these two—Time and Patience." Things might not go as you plan, but work on being patient, careful to tread the remaining steps of love with care. At stake is your whole life, maybe his or hers. Dream that you will be rewarded, and work hard to make the dream a reality.

In the beginning, the rationale is this: if you didn't declare, you are throwing away an unequaled opportunity for happiness. If you didn't state your case, you never will know if there is a chance for a possible relationship. If you didn't take the initiative, you will be denying the opportunity.

This is your ego's most dangerous time.

Lots of thoughts will go through your head before you say anything. You will work through potential rejection, deciding the danger of a bruised ego is worth it. You will wonder if you can suffer the embarrassment if you are rejected, and, if you have true and honorable feelings, you will worry about causing him or her embarrassment.

Perhaps the most you will achieve is friendship. You say you might be in love with this person; he or she might even return the love word; however, you will know it's not romantic love being offered but the kind of love one has for a friend.

Sometimes you will have trouble dealing with that.

Emily Dickinson's poem 1212, "A Word is Dead," reads:

A word is dead
When it is said,
Some say.
I say it just
Begins to live
That day.

I believe that's true. To say the word *love* does not kill it; saying it gives it life and vitality.

Even if your words of love are denied, they were not dead words nor is the emotion killed. Love is energy, love is unity, love is reason to exist.

If a declaration of love is rejected, it's not the word that's rejected, but the messenger. That's tough to take; it's bad enough just contemplating it. But—can you deal with that risk?

You can if the one you love is worthy of your love. The other person may not feel as you do, but you'll never know if you don't take the chance.

It is okay to use the L word.

Say it.

Love!

Reach out, offer your best; if you're fortunate, you'll find truth in Victor Hugo's observation: "The supreme happiness of life is the conviction that we are loved."

Perhaps not loved, not yet. At this step you're opening the potential for love to happen. "Speak for yourself, John." You've done that, timidly perhaps, with subtle skill, I hope. And what a gigantic step this step has been. Never to take that step is self-defeat, is idiotic self-denial, is—. You get my drift.

How do you know the other person is not suffering similar hesitations, is afraid also, and is thinking, "I wish he (or she) would say something?"

How do you know anything until you've been heard and until you listen to the response?

❦ ❦ ❦

Reaching out belies concepts of the ego or the self as a prison from which there is no escape. Theologies, philosophies, and psychologies have long reaffirmed men's (women weren't consulted or considered) ancient beliefs that human existence is tragic because each individual self has been condemned by nature (that is, the gods) to be alone. To believe this, of course, one has to believe that being born, and on top of that being born a human, is in and of itself a tragedy.

Every tragedy ends in death, yet birth and death, two facts of existence, are unchangeable and natural, whether for the stars or for us. Life, in a manner of speaking, is not our birth, which we did not request, or our death, which most of us do not seek, but what happens between birth and death, what we are, what our self, our ego is.

There is some truth to the prison image, but one's prison is self-constructed, bar by restraining bar. "I am alone," the prisoner says. "Focus on me." The self turns inward and says: "There are no others; there is no one of interest except me; only my ideas count; everything is for myself; being concerned about others is weakness; others are the enemy; there is only I against the world."

See the selfish person to know this is true.

For the mentally healthy person, there is a way out of our ego prisons. We are individuals, unique and special and different, single human entities, one of a kind. Does that mean we have to be alone? In one sense, everything is alone: a star, a tree, a toad, a hill, a grain of sand.

However, for humans, because we think and analyze and rationalize, the idea of nature's individualism as a cosmic tragedy, a prison, prevails only when a person allows that notion to exist.

Here's the remarkable fact of human aloneness. When the self reaches out with compassion to another, the prison bands are broken.

Right then. Instantly.

As soon as we make room for another self in our lives, we no longer are alone. Our sense of aloneness disappears immediately,

And when someone cares enough to reach out to us, we have been included. We aren't alone. It's that simple.

When two people reach out for one another, when they create a special bond, when love is exchanged and affirmed, there is no tragedy; there is only togetherness and union—and gladness and joy.

We will speak of ego again. For now let's say simply that reaching out can free you from selfish bondage. You seek another, and if he/she responds to your reach, you are about to experience the riches of life.

To love someone is to wrap him or her in a raiment finer than the most fragile lace and stronger than the thickest armor. Love cannot be seen, yet to be wrapped in it is to be strengthened beyond imagination. Love cannot be seen, yet to be wrapped in it is to be comforted and warmed, given courage and light. Strange, isn't it, that a confluence of emotions with both physical and mental ramifications can move us beyond ourselves into a relationship that in the end is a celebration of ourselves?

Loving

Love with no sense of shame
or regret or remorse.
Love cannot be sullied.
Light innocent love's flame.

This is magic time. You have reached out, spoken, and have received a positive if tentative response.

You've found a special someone; you've declared yourself. Unlike John Alden of old, you didn't rely on a messenger to speak for you; you risked your ego by speaking directly to your intended. And, unlike Cyrano de Bergerac, you didn't resort to subterfuge, speaking your feelings but claiming you were doing so on someone else's behalf.

No—and you weren't rejected out of hand!

You and your declaration of interest, no matter how clumsy and inept, sparked that someone's interest! Bravo! Or at least enough interest to encourage you.

But what—? What if—? What if upon reflection, that special person—?

Rejects you? Gives you the brush-off, the cold shoulder, rebuffs you?

In some dictionaries, "reject" and "rejoice" abut, an ironic, unneighborly pair of words.

Here you are, hoping for a reason to rejoice and realizing you might be a reject, a Loser with a capital L.

We could play with the words, but the possibility is no laughing matter. Rejection is defeat, and if you're rejected, you'll feel lousy, heartbroken, crushed, lifeless, inferior, and a whole lexicon of self-debasing adjectives.

There is no way to defend against rejection. To prepare yourselves against it is negativism, and yet it is the *risk* you must acknowledge and take.

There is no immediate comfort I can give, to you or to myself. We risk, we lose, we suffer. And life goes on. More, life is what we make it and make of it. Love has not been defeated. If we believe in life and love, believing can make life worth living. To believe otherwise is the greatest defeat and failure of all because it means we have given up on life itself.

However, you have not been rejected at this point. How do you proceed? What does it mean to reach out?

Reaching out and *pursuing* are not synonymous. Reaching out toward another is first contact. You've done that, successfully, I hope. Pursuing needs clarification. I've used the word before. It does not mean hunting down, stalking, harassing, or harrying. If there is a way to disprove affection, those activities will do it.

Pursuing as used here, illustrated by the Virginia Bill of Rights and the Declaration of Independence (how's that for authority?), means aspiring to, striving for, questing for happiness.

The seventeenth-century English poet and dramatist John Dryden captured the meaning in these words:

'Tis not for nothing that we life pursue;
It pays our hopes with something still that's new.
—*Aurengzebe,* act 4. scene 1.

Pursuing, striving to keep, questing for the affection of the individual of your dreams is a lifelong task. We'll speak more of this later, but it seems wise to say this much now: to really love someone means you must prove it every day, and that means giving as much thought and attention to love and loving a year from now and ten years from now and a hundred years from now as you do at this moment.

There's the old Jimmy Walker song, "Will You Love Me in December as You Do in May?" Skeptics say the former mayor of New York City was polling the voters, but the song was written long before debonair Jimmy got into politics.

The question is legitimate, though, even if Jimmy wasn't always, because loving is a full-time job: the total commitment of one's self to another—forever.

If you must have more, jump ahead to the words about *committing.* For now, at least, be clear in your mind. Reaching out is a single episode; pursuing your loved one is a life-long commitment.

Art, music, literature—great or mediocre, joyful or vindictive—created out of hate or despair or love, are designed to influence the viewer, the hearer, or the reader. So, too, with the words and physical expressions of love; you are trying to convey your best self and your truest feelings, wanting to convince *that certain other,* "I am the best because of you and for you."

❦ ❦ ❦

Reaching out took courage, didn't it? In matters of the heart, seniors seem to lack courage. Oh, courage isn't the right word. I think confidence is the word. Simply put, you've been out of the romance loop for a time; lack of confidence and self-doubt will temper your thoughts and actions.

That's why we're considering the steps of love one at a time, to refresh our memories about what real love is, realigning our loving selves by remembering not only how we ought to behave but why, and presenting our best, thoughtful, caring, considerate, loving selves to that *special other.*

If making a good first impression was hard, establishing, maintaining, and strengthening the bonds of love will be much harder. Remember, if you truly love someone, you're in love for the long haul.

You survived the awkward first encounter. Now you really have to go to work. To declare love is a lot easier than proving it.

❦ ❦ ❦

Before we proceed, this is a good place to remind ourselves we don't love a person because he or she is perfect.

Once, a man told me his fiancée, apparently harboring some doubts, kept asking him why he loved her. Something was missing from his list of reasons. Some intangible idea she sought and didn't hear; something she needed to feel was absent.

We love someone because in some mysterious, often inexplicable, interaction of emotions that person brings something wonderful to our lives, something that is received from no other. That *something* gives us a sense of worth, of completeness, of wholeness, a sense that with that person all things are possible.

When I spoke with the woman, that's what was missing, the promise that her man's love was strong enough to make her perfect. His love reasons focused on himself, and that was natural.

It was not enough.

It took a long time to get him to realize completely that what he wanted to receive he had to give. The day I asked him if his fiancée was perfect was his day of awakening. "No," he said, "she's not perfect, but I can give her the strength and encouragement to be whatever she wants to become."

"As she gives you encouragement and strength?"

"Yes."

"Then why not tell her?"

"Tell her what?"

"That you love her for what and who she is, for what she is going to help you become, for what, whatever that is, she will become because of you, because loving her is the promise that tomorrow both of you will be richer and stronger, that together all things are possible. Tell her your life is devoted to her. Once she feels the truth of that, she'll need no other reassurances."

The poet E. E. Cummings penned this profound truth: "We do not believe in ourselves until someone reveals that deep inside us something is valuable, worth listening to, worthy of our trust, sacred to the touch." The man's fiancée needed to feel that revelation.

❦   ❦   ❦

Years ago I read a letter written as a spoof. It went something like this: "Dear Lass, I love you. With you I could climb the highest mountain, swim the broadest ocean, wrestle the biggest bear, fly above the clouds. Love, Harry.

"P.S. If it doesn't rain tomorrow, I'll be over."

Poor Harry, his euphoria wasn't matched by his weak reality; he was afraid of getting his feet wet or catching cold.

When we present ourselves, we present our best selves, not perfect selves. And what we wish for in return is not a perfect partner. Our hope is at once both simple and endlessly profound: that together we will make each other more perfect, that the partnership will strengthen our good qualities and lead each toward perfection.

In what started out as a casual conversation following a community meeting, a woman I barely knew asked if it was okay for a wife to give her husband a list of his faults. Fault listing was in vogue at the time, thanks to a number of misguided magazine and TV treatments of marital difficulties. When I expressed doubt that the exchange in and of itself would produce anything creative, she expressed her doubt as to my insight—or lack of it.

I offered my opinion that before being so openly confrontational there was substantial groundwork to be done if the need to enumerate faults was present.

Apparently the need was present and outweighed the woman's doubts.

When the couple entered my office, both appeared apprehensive. That's not uncommon. Who wants to air difficulties in front of a stranger? They were civil, even congenial at times. They had, they said, agreed on two ground rules. They would be honest and what they said was not meant to hurt the other. Each wanted their marriage to continue; each acknowledged it had become stale and flat.

The wife wanted to read her list of her husband's faults. "Before you do that," I said, "I want you to make another list. I want you to list your own faults." I gave each a piece of paper and a pencil.

Reluctantly, they complied. Neither wrote much, I noticed.

I asked the wife to read from the list she had just written. Without allowing the husband to respond, I asked her to read the prepared list of her husband's faults. There were few real faults; most of her list were annoyances, a couple of which would have annoyed me, too.

Two or three faults she said she might possess were also on the list of her husband's faults. I mentioned them.

Without further comment, I had the husband read from his list of what he thought were his faults. Some matched faults his wife found with him.

When I asked for his list of his wife's faults, he didn't have one. "I love my wife," he declared. "If she has faults, I don't see them. She isn't perfect, but I think she is."

That was the first time I heard that sentiment expressed. I've heard it a few times since but never often enough.

He went on, looking at the floor. "In my real estate business, everything is location, location, location. In my marriage, it should be I love you, I love you, I love you. The other side of it is, she loves me, she loves me, she loves me."

Now we were ready to deal with the faults, but the wife beat me to it.

She tore up her list. "There's only one fault," she said. "I don't hear the love word often enough. And I don't speak it when I should." She reached out and took her husband's hand.

We did talk, about imperfection and trust, openness and ego, communication and all the rest, what they had once and almost let slip away. They never returned. I suppose they learned to deal with her short temper and his squeezing the toothpaste tube in the middle, his habit of leaving dirty clothes on the floor and her need to have help with the dinner dishes, his attraction to TV football and her attraction to more cultural happenings.

Only in the imagination are there "perfect" partners. Being in love should mean being aware of one's messiness and correcting it, or one's short fuse and lengthening it, or one's proclivity to annoy and ceasing whatever it is that annoys. Sometimes we get too comfortable with or take for granted the love we receive. Imperfect to begin with, we become more so. Love isn't supposed to work that way.

🍂 🍂 🍂

Love is the most untainted thought we can express. From its many levels, from agape (altruism, charity, service) to eros (ardor, "the hots," passion), true love is honest and selfless. Even in passion, true love seeks mutuality and shared union—and reciprocity. To love someone is to place that someone's welfare above one's own, to help one's loved one achieve new heights beyond one's own. There is no *me first* in love. In this sense, the opposite of love is not unlove or lack of love; certainly it is not hate; in this context, the opposite of love is selfishness and ego building at the expense of the other.

You know that. Do you know what to do with that knowledge?

As a thought, love has no opposite. One loves or one does not love. It's at the emotional, visceral level that the yin-yang nature of opposites applies, the pain-pleasure circle in which most of us exist. That's why love is portrayed so often as something painful. Having love, giving or receiving it, gives us pleasure; it's the absence of love that gives us pain.

We seek the pleasures that love can bring; that's natural. Pleasure at the expense of a partner is selfishness; in no way can that be called love. Pleasure comes from outside, in this instance from someone. Joy or happiness comes from within.

🍂 🍂 🍂

If you think love is for the young only, then you've died before you're dead. If you think old or older people cannot love, you don't deserve love. The whole idea of loving isn't for you.

If you think people will make fun of you behind your back, or be embarrassed for you, or be scandalized by your romantic relationship, or wonder if you have all your marbles, ignore them.

Ignore children who think you are insane, too. They won't love you any less, but they might ask if you're ready for the farm for strange folks. In no uncertain words assure them that you are not ready for the great pasture and that you have a whole life yet to live. They will understand.

What possible shame is there in loving someone? Sometimes children view their parent's new love affair as a betrayal of the deceased or separated parent. Unless there is something untoward in it, the problem is the children's, not yours. Rest assured, while they may think you took too many coconuts to the head, they will continue to love and respect you. And they will support you because your happiness is important to them.

You will ask yourself questions, and you must answer honestly. If you love someone or have great affection for someone, if you hope for a lasting and romantic relationship, can you, for your part, establish and maintain a relationship without regret or remorse?

Let me give an example of regret and remorse, one that's more complicated than the above paragraph would suggest but illustrative of the kinds of problems loving the second time around can produce.

A man I had assisted years earlier called and asked if he could come to see me. Years before I had helped his family work through some problems involving his children. He sought my help again.

As his wife was dying, he said, she made him promise he would not remarry. He made the promise. Except when he was in the army, he continued, he and his wife made love every single night of their marriage, almost fifty years. They did not always engage in intercourse, but they held, fondled, aroused, and comforted each other. The love they voiced in the daylight they expressed physically at night.

"My wife made me promise not to remarry; she said I could [go to bed with] as many women as I wanted as long as I didn't marry one of them."

The problem he brought was not complicated. He had found someone he wanted to marry. And he had made a promise.

"What do you want from me?" I asked.

"I want your permission to marry the woman."

"You don't need my permission."

"But I do."

"You want me to tell you it's okay to break your promise?"

"Yes."

"The woman knows you've made the promise?"

"She wonders why I can't marry her."

My friend's ethical problem, as he saw it, was dooming his future happiness. To live with his newfound love without benefit of marriage was a moral compromise. He didn't say and I didn't ask whether he was sleeping with her; that was irrelevant. He had loved his wife; now he loved another. There was one impediment: the promise.

I told him there was a concept of law that held deathbed conversations to be without legal standing, and I asked him if his late wife's request for his promise might have been more a need for the reassurance of his love than for prohibition.

He hadn't thought about that.

Permission to remarry? I wanted to give that even though my permission was meaningless. Anyway, I knew that wasn't what he wanted. He wanted support, absolution even, for breaking a promise. I could give support; I couldn't grant the guilt-free conscience he sought.

"I'll help you find a rationale," I told him, "but the answer to your dilemma is somewhere in your own mind." "If you break what you perceive as an ironclad promise," I continued, "you will never totally be able to love your new wife. Always there will be regret that you broke the promise, and remorse. Either solve the ethical question in your own mind or forsake marriage. If you don't come to terms with your [late] wife's demand, you will be miserable and your new wife will be miserable."

I recommended he see a psychotherapist who practiced in my friend's city. I urged him to make an appointment.

As he left, I told him, "Do what is right for you, in your mind and in your heart."

The injunction, "Let the dead bury the dead," is relevant here, part of the next step. Whatever my friend did, as I saw it, his decision and consequent actions neither helped nor harmed his late wife.

I understood his wife's request. In one form or another, it's a request made often by spouses who wish to die emotionally wrapped in an aura of lasting love. And because of that, sometimes we make promises, not to keep but to comfort someone we love.

What concerned me most in that day's consultation was the great potential for harm to my friend and to his new loved one.

If—and a big if it was—his wife intended to dirty or soil any future love affair, she succeeded. I doubt she intended that result; I think she loved my friend enough to let him go, hoping that he would be fulfilled, sexually as she allowed, and in all other ways. That's what true love wants.

My friend did not remarry; he and his new woman did carry on a meaningful and fulfilling love affair. In that he compromised, and he kept his promise, sometimes choking on it, but with his integrity intact.

I assume, I do not know for certain, that because the second woman loved him, she accommodated his difficult indecision, loving him but never totally having him, her burden. For a long time I wondered if he ever revealed the reason he wouldn't remarry. I'll never know. He died just before I finished this book.

Real love is without subterfuge, is innocent of harboring dark secret "deals." The chapter on "Banishing/

Renouncing" deals with our pasts, issues that must be handled by the two people involved. And I hasten to add that there are items from the past that must be allowed to stay there. Unfortunately for my friend, a past item loomed large in the present and directly affected the future of two people.

❦ ❦ ❦

To turn to another thought, when things go wrong in the world or personal affairs become sticky and difficult to resolve, I have an acquaintance who sometimes likes to quotes Wordsworth (he of the one-sided love affair with his sister), "The world is too much with us."

It's a rare human being who hasn't bemoaned that fact. In my role as a counselor, I used to hear the sentiment most often from those who, for all intents and purposes, were single. The husband, wife, closest friend, lover was distant and unsupportive. Although that person was physically present, still there was no one upon whom to lean, no one with whom to share the struggle to keep an even keel, no one to counterbalance depression or the blues. Conversely, when life served up a few cherries, there was no one with whom to share the joy, no one with whom to sing the songs, no one with whom to dance to the rhythmic heartbeat of life.

Fortunate is the man or woman who has a loving partner with whom to share life's ups and downs.

You are the would-be lover and your arms must embrace your loved one both during life's struggles and in life's victories. It's been said before, as arms entwine the bodies, so does love bind two hearts together.

Entwine. Bind together. That's what we hope will happen.

❦ ❦ ❦

I'm going to take a detour at this point. "Fortunate is the man or woman who has a loving partner...." That's what I said three paragraphs ago, and that's what I mean. How many times have you heard, "My friends provide all the love I need?"

For some people that may be true; more may claim its truth. For many, however, no matter how large a cadre of friends one has, friends do not provide the support, partnership, and intimate one-to-one relationship that a loving partner provides. A partner is the alter ego that builds up our own.

It is one thing to have loving arms hold us when we are down and loving arms to embrace us when we celebrate our joys; to some extent, friends do that, and we bless them for it. But a loving partner does more. A loving partner is there, day and night, making your plans his or hers, bearing your sorrows, comforting you, encouraging you. A loving partner knows when you need a hug or a kiss and eagerly awaits your private expressions of unity. It may sound corny, but in the words of the old song *Danny Boy,* "in sunshine or sorrow ... because I love you so." Friends do the showy things; a loving partner takes out the garbage or sews on a button. A friend pats your shoulder; a loving partner holds your hand. Friends smile in joy or pout in sorrow; a loving partner cries your tears and laughs your victories.

Oh, we need friends. The best of all possible worlds is

when our loved one is also our best friend. Probably we
don't crawl into bed with our friends; with our loved
one we do, there at the end of the day, to cuddle and
soothe and repledge the love we have tried to express
throughout the day.

♥   ♥   ♥

It's essential at this point to say more about friends
and friendships. If you and your intended partner enjoy
the congeniality of the same social group, then your
friendships-in-common will be secure. But if you have
come together from out of separate social circles, one of
your obligations is to include your new partner in your
friendship circle, and, a second obligation, to be
included willingly in a new circle of potential friends.

There is joy in fulfilling those obligations. Not only
are both your worlds expanded, each has an opportunity
to make and develop new friendships.

Your new personal relationship does not and should
not imply withdrawal from friends. Including your partner in your friendships—and being included in his or
her friendships—will, in the long run, only strengthen
your relationship.

Sometimes people worry unnecessarily that because
one has a romantic friend, old friends will be jealous.
Seldom is that true. Friends will be happy for you. At
the same time, you will, by maintaining your friendships, reassure your friends of their continued importance in your life.

No matter how intense the relationship, a loving
partner recognizes the importance of the other's friend-

ships and encourages and insists on their continuance. To be in love with someone does not mean to withdraw from the world. You will have your private moments; friends will respect them.

Having someone important in your life does mean adjustments. On the one hand, if love is real, adjustments will be made. On the other hand, if friendships are true, adjustments will be made, too. Unless there is something unhealthy about one's love or friendships, everyone will be richer and happier.

♥ ♥ ♥

When I was a child there were few role models. Perhaps it was the lack of expressed affection in my dysfunctional home or the fallout of certain Victorian mores; we practiced "convention" even if our heart wasn't in it, when, compared to today, there was a much different view of the opposite sex and how one behaved toward and with a boy or a girl we liked.

We learned our behavior from literature and movies, not from our parents and grandparents. Mostly we learned to look and not touch. We "courted" a girl or were courted by a boy; engagements might last for years before marriage; there was a value to virginity; allegedly, "cold showers" were common. Women are quick to remind me that boys had sports for sublimation; women had needle point and tatting, poor substitutes.

Skip a few generations and it's "Hello, whatever your name is; where's the bedroom?" A novel or a movie that doesn't have a hot and sweaty lovemaking scene doesn't get very far.

There's a not so subtle difference between loving someone, that is, emotionally reaching out to that someone, and making love, the physical, intimate contact of your body with another's. Here we are speaking of love, not lovemaking. It is the wise senior person who knows the difference and can separate the two.

For seniors, virginity is seldom an issue (although there are other issues to consider). Chastity, in the various meanings of the word, may be an issue, as may modesty or abstention or self-control or self-denial. Somewhere between the absolute cold "no" and the passionate hot "yes" without regard for anything except the sex act, there is a balance point, one each individual and couple must find.

Sexual activity, in and of itself, is not love. The "If you loved me, you would…" plea has been around since time began. Having intimate sex is a natural, desirable consequence of being in love. But—and a gigantic "but" it is—if you wish your new relationship to last, it must be built on more fundamental things than engaging in sex.

Trust, respect, caring, sharing are the foundations of a union. It's not without reason it's been said over and over again that the biggest turn-on is a man cleaning windows or a woman preparing a pie.

There's no point belaboring the issue: if you want to light a flame of love, first you love and demonstrate your love in many little ways and then you have sex. The sex act seldom generates love. That's a hard lesson to learn, but it is true.

There's no question: seniors are consenting adults, whatever they do. If anything was learned from earlier relationships, it's that "paving the way" to whatever we hope to achieve is strenuous and diligent work. Loving in all its nuances means we present ourselves and create the climate or atmosphere in a way that physical expressions of our love are the natural, desired extension of the care that leads to them. Making love is an end one may seek; it's not the other way around.

For now, like it or not, we're dealing with love, not making love. The moral question, whether to engage in intercourse, is yours alone. By that I mean the plural *your*. You and your loved one agree to decide mutually and to abide by the decision.

The moral/emotional issues are important and we will deal with them in the chapter on lovemaking. For now, if you are active, it must be by mutual consent, without fear of sinfulness or contrary to your moral standard. If you are hesitant or unsure, a loving partner will understand. He or she may not like it, but understanding will come.

Lovemaking by mutual consent. That's what love implies: shared thoughts, shared goals, shared activities, unison, togetherness, harmony, balance.

❦ ❦ ❦

A final thought: when you give love, you give the most precious gift you have; you give yourself.

Responding positively to the gift of love is your gift to the giver.

No exchange of gifts is greater than giving and

receiving love. Nor is any exchange more laden with responsibilities. Delmore Schwartz titled one of his short stories "In Dreams Begins Responsibilities." While the story is inappropriate here, the title is not. Now you're dreaming for two. Giving love is giving your whole self into someone else's care; accepting love is accepting that person's whole care. That someone becomes the most important person in your life, more important than you yourself, an awesome responsibility.

If your dream is for a lifelong union with the one you love, the responsibility is accepted eagerly and executed with devoted care. It will not even be seen as a responsibility; it will be thought of as privilege and opportunity, love's mutual blessing.

Banishing/Renouncing

Heed not doubt from yesterday
nor future fear. In love
all things are possible;
love provides its own way.

Render to limbo's death
the ego, illusions,
expectations: in love
the death of these is breath.

You've come a long way. You've met someone; you
might even be falling in love. Perhaps you are in love.

Happy days?

Maybe.

Maybe not.

Banishing and *renouncing* might be viewed as one giant
step or as two entirely separate tiny twin steps. Or
maybe they are the same step seen in two different ways.
You'll be aware of differences and similarities, so I'll
leave the distinction to you. I have segregated them, and
yet I acknowledge they often are taken simultaneously,
because one has to do with doubt and fear and the other
with ego.

Confused? Don't be. When we were younger, we
climbed stairs two at a time. The steps we skipped were
important; we just didn't need them at the time. Now
they are there when we do need them. They support us

on our journey toward completeness.

Perhaps your earlier marriage or relationship was so grand you doubt another will fulfill you. Or perhaps to the contrary, your previous relationship was so terrible you doubt a new, deep relationship can bring you happiness.

Anyone who had a precious spouse or domestic partner is to be envied; such a relationship is wonderful. Cherish the memories. Near perfect mates or partners will not be replaced. Only a domineering control freak would seek to replace your former loved partner. Whether you are the loving one or the loved one, no one should attempt to destroy or eliminate the past's grand memories.

By the same token, a new partner should not be considered a replacement or a substitute. Substitutes have the connotation of being of lesser quality and temporary, certainly not what you would want to be or would accept.

A new partner will be or will try to be new and fresh and loving, and if the partner is, then a brand new union will be created, not replacing the good life ended but extending both lives into unique, new, unexplored areas of their own.

The words "unique" and "unexplored" are chosen deliberately. The possibility of a second chance for love implies that with a new, other person your whole life will change. You should welcome the difference. The uniqueness of your new friend will lead you in eager anticipation to the unexplored (and renewed) life that lies ahead.

In a 1936 letter to her mother, Anaïs Nin wrote, "Each friend represents a world to us, a world possibly not born until they arrive, and it is only by this meeting that a new world is born."

Such a profound truth—if we allow ourselves to enter that new world.

♥   ♥   ♥

If your former relationship was less than happy, was abusive, demeaning, or humiliating, you will have doubts about yourself and about the hidden dangers in any long relationship. You will doubt or not quite trust any potential partner.

Whether you are the sender or the receiver of love thoughts, an earlier relationship of alienation can leave you angry, confused, and possessed of self-pity, to say nothing of being anxious and cynical.

To use a phrase, perhaps you have put your negative experiences on the back burner where anxiety and fear simmer. Consequently, you may withhold intimacy, not just physical but emotional, and you may have difficulty achieving meaningful compatibility.

If you let it, a less than satisfactory former marriage or relationship can disable you.

Sometimes one of two disabling consequences follows the dissolution of a less than wholesome partnership. One is a kind of guilty relief that the partnership is dissolved, followed months later by an irrational need to defend, praise, and extol the departed partner. "Josh" or "Nancy," the abuser, gradually becomes pure and solid gold. If the abusive partner has died, mourning comes much later, sometimes years later. The abuse is consigned to the past; the good things are brought into the present, and guilt moves one to recount the good, denying the bad.

Or, unless one is narcissistic or deep into denial, one questions his or her own responsibility and/or fault, defending the dead, as it were.

In either case, at the least is a lack of self-confidence; at worst is a guilt difficult or impossible to bear.

It is so unnecessary—if you can consign the past to the past. If there were mistakes, they have been committed; if there were faults, they have been recognized; if there were deeds of commission or omission, they and all the other possible failures are of the past. To dwell on them is fruitless; to learn from them is wisdom. For the emotionally healthy person, the time for blaming and excusing has passed. A new day is dawning.

Easier said than done. If you are carrying doubts and fears into a new relationship, express them and discuss them. Not only can you and your new partner deal with them at least to the extent that the partner is aware of them, revealing your doubts and fears helps the other person know who and what you are.

For example: "I loved my husband; he died." "My wife cheated on me." "My girlfriend beat the children." "My lover abused me." "He was a drunk [or a druggie or a gambler]."

Sometimes feelings of doubt and fear are not based on such obvious reasons but are a buildup of less dramatic shortcomings. Nonetheless, they jaundice any new relationship and sometimes they prevent it entirely.

Love might be, can be, but is not guaranteed to be, the catalyst that sets you free.

Free is a relative word. If you were in a bad marriage, somewhere along the way you became stoic, suffering in silence, gutting it out, finally withdrawing into your own shell. In the home, there was no support. You either sought it elsewhere or absented yourself as often as you could.

Loving someone does not make all hurts disappear. Some will remain with you for the rest of your life. Loving someone and having someone love you in return provides a helpmate who will listen sympathetically, share your distress, and give you the emotional support you need to overcome or at least bear the truculent pain. But even then, some of that pain will remain.

Of all the things love can be, the most meaningful is sharing hopes and joys, fears and sorrows. To a degree, friends do that; lovers (more than casual intimate partners) extend their sharing from the highest ecstasy to the deepest anguish. Casual sex partners never share your pain.

With one who loves you, you are never alone; you face your world together with your partner; you have someone who knows your earlier pain.

What relationship could be more sublime?

A caution: no prospective partner wants to hear about or needs to know about former lovers. It's one thing to reveal episodes from a marriage; they help establish your ground rules and reveal your emotional needs. It's quite another thing to reveal temporary love affairs. In this regard, separate your life into two parts, before you met your new love and after that meeting. Romantic affairs in the past should remain there, untold; your whole focus should be on the present and the future. Nothing is gained by revealing trysts; there is everything to lose.

Even in this day and age of open and uncensored sexual conversation, no one wants to hear, "I haven't had a man for a while" or "You're bigger (or smaller) than J—" or "C— liked...." Certainly don't compare your new partner with your former or late spouse or domestic partner, certainly not with a former temporary or casual lover. Such statements will wrap any possible romance in an impenetrable haze of emotional pollution. Misused, the past can soil the present and spoil the future.

Your entire focus should be on your loved one, and even though you and the loved one know differently, this love should be acted out as if it was the first: the first hug, the first kiss, the first intimate contact.

T. S. Eliot in his "Four Quartets," wrote, "We shall not cease from exploration," That line continues with:

> And the end of all our exploring
> Will be to arrive where we started
> And know the place for the first time.

I doubt our lives to be perfect circles, the end returning to the beginning, but I do believe, as Eliot suggests, that we meet all rediscoveries for the first time. Should we fall in love a second time, it will be an entirely new and awesome adventure of exploration and must be treated as such.

To put it bluntly, treat the loving experience as brand new for both of you. And in their way, the little white lie not withstanding, each touch and kiss is brand new. You have a new partner; there is wonder in learning about your new partner, and exotic mystery in discovering your new love, and pleasure in learning to please and be pleased. It is a brand new beginning not to be clouded by events from the past.

"Love will find a way" is misleading and sentimental, open to question. Regardless of the nature of your past, all memories are tinged by melancholy; there is regret, sorrow, bitter joy, doubt. There's a sadness born of the past. Even the great memories have their sadness because they didn't last. A worthy partner and lover will hold you and lick the tears from your cheeks. And if you are among the fortunate, your partner's sight and sound and taste will help banish your sadness and fears.

Love by itself does not find the way; you and he, you and she, will find a way—together.

❦ ❦ ❦

I always smile when I think of comedian Fred Allen's line, "The last time I saw him he was walking down Lover's Lane holding his own hand." It draws a perfect picture of the supreme egoist. It's hard to imagine such a person loving any other person; if he or she did, pity the other.

There are levels (or kinds, if you prefer) of ego. There

is the concept of self as different from others, unique, of individual worth, with all the ego thoughts and behaviors that in our daily lives makes self-preservation our central concern. That's basic to human survival. A sound and balanced ego is essential to one's concept of the cosmos and life and our place and role in both. Our individual lives, for us, are central to everything and everyone around us. To be concerned about ourselves is natural and normal.

There are two less-than-healthy facets of egotism, however. One is the sense of one's lack of worth, the sense of personal failure, of being less than we might be, physically, mentally, and emotionally.

The other is being so egocentric that the self is total conceit, selfish and narcissistic, in French, *amour propre.*

For the egocentric person, love is doomed to failure. Love serves only the egoist without regard for the partner; the partner never will be fully a part of the egoist's heart and mind.

For certain, I am the center of my world: I am the one who perceives it, reacts to it, plans for myself in it, finds reality in it. That is true for every individual. We are our own selves, and self plus self plus self adds up to the world's population, each self the center, each self an individual of potential worth, each self seeking to fulfill his or her basic life needs.

There is nothing wrong with that. It is natural in the way of human life. The trouble comes when one's ego does not recognize or cannot make room for other selves.

Giving up ego is a misnomer. It does not mean giving up on yourself or denying your individual importance; it means giving up your egocentricity (me, alone) and opening your heart to include another.

In the best of worlds, people do that. It's called agape, charity, kindness, compassion, love. It is what cements together humane societies and makes us civilized.

In a loving partnership, one ego makes room for another ego, and each takes on the task of providing the basic needs of the other.

Think of it this way: the selves are separate circles yet they overlap and become one larger circle, illustrated spiritually and artistically by the Taoist yin-yang symbol and by the Ute Indian circles touching circles within the larger circle.

In love it's not *if* your ego can meld with and include the circle of another, it's that it *must*, else love cannot happen.

When our ego does accommodate another ego, a wondrous thing happens. The center of life shifts from *me* to *us*. There is more than *I*; there is *we*. You say to your ego, "Expand! Make room for the other." Is your ego diminished when you do that? Quite the opposite. It grows because now you have another in the center of your life, one whose welfare is as much a concern as your own. And blessedly, you have become central to and in another life. You are in good hands with a good heart that loves you.

In Abraham Maslow's theory, love and being loved (accepted) are vital to one's achievement of a healthy self-actualization. And that works both ways, for you and for the one you love.

And as I've suggested, a wonderful thing happens. When your ego makes room for another ego, your ego circle doesn't get crowded, it expands! You need that special someone, and when you make room for that person, your ego space and the whole world grows larger.

The psychoanalyst Carl Gustav Jung, whose sometime patient was the American writer Anaïs Nin (quoted in the last chapter), wrote, "Where love rules, there is no will to power, and where power predominates, there love is lacking." The power seeking, selfish, meanly ego must die, else, if love is present, it will wither, or if love is conceived, it will be stillborn.

"The meeting of two personalities" Jung said, "is like the contact of two chemical substances: if there is any reaction, both are transformed." You know that is true. You haven't come this far without an overwhelming awareness of something happening in your life, to your life and within you. You are being transformed, changed, in wondrous ways.

❦   ❦   ❦

Here a word for those whose fragile egos have been knocked about by life, who doubt their own worth, who believe their lives to be failures.

A healthy ego is believing in one's self. From before our first steps, from before our successful toilet training, from before our first attempts to speak words, from before our first smile, from our birth, if we were lucky, if we were loved, someone encouraged us and urged us to accomplish great things, to turn over, to crawl, to hold a spoon, to learn the alphabet, to sleep without a light. Always the efforts; always the praise. We could do it.

But for many of us, when we were much too young, those who believed in us left us on our own. They didn't die; they simply stopped parenting, and the unfortunate consequence was, when we sought to be worthy, there was no one to tell us how valuable we were, no one to listen to us, no one who trusted our judgment, no one who wrapped an arm around our shoulders and praised and encouraged us.

Our egos, needing confirmation, were abandoned. We didn't believe in ourselves because we thought no one believed in us. And sadly for too many, the sense of being unrecognized was compounded in marriage; one's spouse simply did not know enough to encourage and praise his or her mate or, worse, simply didn't care. One has only to consider so-called domestic abuse to know the truth. One partner believes the other to be worthless and, ultimately, regards that other as a nonperson.

One's ego deflated and/or defeated, there's little middle ground. Mostly we're either burdened by a sense of inferiority ("No matter how hard I try, I just can't....") or we become insufferably arrogant ("The world is rotten; it's me against everybody."). Either way, the ego is on the defensive.

The overblown, intolerable (to everyone else) ego is a defensive posture. In military terms it's "first strike;" in corporate terms it's "acquire at all costs;" in social and political terms it's "me first." It's not pretty. A self-love that denies all others is incapable of meaningful, affectionate relationships because always trust is absent. Any love affair will be short lived. No one can long survive the selfish onslaught.

My sense of the defeated, the sense of inferiority, the shattered ego is that they result not from failure as such but from disappointment. Something went wrong, so blame yourself. You say you weren't wise enough, strong enough, skillful enough. Most of us aren't; most of us accept the risk of failure as the potential result of trying. Failure is our great disappointment because we are disappointed in ourselves. It's not the failure per se that nags us. Our disappointment is in our lack of strength, our lack of skill, our lack of wisdom.

Failure is no crime. We beat up on ourselves needlessly. "I'm not good enough" often is surrender. We stop trying. "I'm too old; I'm too fat; I'm not pretty any more; I'm incapable of feeling; I wouldn't know how to act." All excuses, all expressions of self-disappointment, all little white flags of capitulation, all saying, "I don't think I can; I don't want to disappoint myself again, so I won't try."

How sad. We've talked about consigning the past to the past. That's where failures belong. Yes, it's true, you may fail again, but never to take that risk is to live the rest of your life posthumously.

Besides, you've got support, arms, and a heart to sustain you, and you've got someone who cares about you, lovingly and passionately. There is a future to be grasped even by those who once saw no meaningful future.

❦ ❦ ❦

In love there are few great expectations beyond giving your whole self and hoping for a whole self in return, and if that happens, then work hard to ensure that both selves are fulfilled. It's in the togetherness, the sharing, the common concerns and endeavors where love is expressed most eloquently and deeply.

It is true: to be understood, with all your fears and doubts, is to be accepted for who and what you are, and to seek the understanding of another is to express your deep love.

Love is not expressed in power or domination; a lover does not rule the roost; there is no love in *me, me.* Someone has pointed out that there is no *I* in the words "team" or "together."

And it is wise to repeat this truth: love is not always smooth. Disagreements and contrary ideas are inevitable. They do not negate love. But unless they are confronted head on and resolved, they can and will strain any relationship. Loving the one who disagrees with you means precisely that. You may dislike the contrary idea; you do not love the holder of that idea less.

If your ego is intact and if your ego has made room for and has embraced the other, no disagreement threatens separation. Love provides room for disagreement. If you love truly, no disagreement can do you any harm. If you do not love well, no agreement will do you much good.

True love means resolving disagreements creatively.

And if creatively means compromise, then compromise. Stuff your ego in your pocket. Winning at all costs is to lose; winning for the sake of winning is just plain stupid. Compromise is an art. Each believes he or she is loved enough to receive the larger or greater consideration.

Listening is an art. Unfortunately, there are too few good artists. Whatever you do, heed this advice. When you begin to argue, you've stopped listening. Your partner may be expressing some very stupid thoughts; arguing will only elicit more of the same. You know, the more stupid you are, the more defensive you become— and the more you prove that defensive stupidity can be a terminal disease. I could illustrate; let's just say I've done that.

I think we were given two ears and only one mouth because listening is twice as important as speaking. Nothing must block communication between two loved ones. One heart listening to another heart is, in the curious way of human behavior, the voicing of love. *I hear you* bespeaks love. Let no words deny you or your loved one that.

Planning

Yield the past to the past;
build on the good, forgive
the bad; rendezvous with
the new day, future vast.

Without becoming too philosophical, whatever has led us to this point is in the past: misfortune, suffering, the nexus of guilt and doom, all the tragic "epics" the finite person experiences, and accomplishments, joys, the nexus of love and hope, all the wondrous episodes a finite person experiences.

When we were young, being finite, if that thought ever occurred to us, was of no concern. As Andy Rooney said once, "Death is just a distant rumor to the young." Life, we thought—although probably we knew better—was forever.

For seniors, finite has its limits. Life is not endless; we know, no matter how well we veil it or seek to deny it, mortality will engulf us and our achievements and successes. So some say, what's the use, why try, we're all headed for the grave.

Mostly nonsense. The end of our lives is inevitable, that's true, but.... All the more reason to make good use of the vigorous life that's left, to wring from the remaining years all the sweet juice of life we can.

To state the issue dramatically, we can drown ourselves in the flood of our tears or we can toss our hopes into the pool of despair and cause a tiny ripple of hopeful love to reach from shore to shore. Enough ripples will become a flow, and on the flow of hope, we can sail to the successful, joyful conclusion of our life voyage.

The morning after I wrote the preceding paragraph, my newspaper carried an article, "More Americans are Dying...of Old Age," which struck me as a farcical, slapstick burlesque joke.

There used to be a comedy routine in which a youngster is asked, "And how old would you be?" And the child replies, "I don't know; I haven't lived that long yet." When the knowledgeable laughter died down, it was followed with, "But I'm older than I used to be." More laughter, because that's everyone's answer.

Of course we're dying of old age; that comes with living longer. We don't need inane newspaper fillers to tell us that. Look at the numbers. Actuaries tell us that someone sixty-five can, statistically (in 2005), expect to live another eighteen years. Those older can make their own estimate. Or, they can purchase a Life Expectancy Watch, advertised to "actually count backward, keeping you apprised of your forthcoming expiration date" based on data about your age and lifestyle.

I had a friend who lived into his late nineties, and when I say lived, I mean robustly and vigorously. At his ninetieth birthday party he told everyone that when he died, and if he was reincarnated, he wanted to come back as a woman. "I'm doing everything a man can do," he said; "I'd like to do everything a woman can do."

When someone asked if that meant giving birth, he

answered, "Oh, yes. I had a kidney stone, so I know pain. What I'd like to do is be the giver of life."

The years available to us can be a whole new lifetime. In this sense, I'd rather have one impeccable and mind-blowing moment of true happiness than numberless moments of mere pleasure.

A recent on-line computer survey asked if users would rather have a period of intense happiness which when over would be completely forgotten as though it never happened, or would users rather continue their present search for happiness, assuming they had not achieved that goal.

I checked the happiness box. Then I unchecked it. At first I thought I'd give everything for happiness; then I wondered what good it would be if I couldn't remember having been happy.

If I was going to live only as long as that happy period lasted, that would be my choice, hands down. But what if I achieved happiness and didn't know it? What if, by some magic, happiness came without any effort on my part? Who or what would decide what my happiness was to be? I decided I'd rather continue my own search, even knowing I might never achieve that precious time. But, if I did....

I agree with Robert G. Ingersoll: "Happiness is the only good.... The way to be happy is to make others so." Never is that more truthful for seniors than when they are in love. Stephen Covey defines vision as "the ability to see beyond our present reality, to create, to invent what does not yet exist, to become what we not yet are."

Many stories don't have happy endings. Such endings as "they lived happily ever after," we have to create.

So you have discovered and reached out to someone. You are in love. You've cleared your mind, dealt with your doubts, faced your fears. You sense potential happiness in a lasting love affair. *Me* has become *us*; *I* has become *we*. You are striving as hard as you can to become the friend, partner, lover you think your loved one wants and needs and deserves. You are becoming what you not yet are, a pair, a couple, a *we*.

But your new love may be hesitant, not fully in love, not ready to make *the commitment*, not able to banish fears, not entirely conquering doubts.

Take heart; be your best; let the future take its course.

Planning for the future is not the same as predetermining the future. When I was in public school, teachers had a compulsive fixation on outlines. To get to D, the conclusion, one had to know A, where we started, and then carefully identify points B and C in between. That made for good compositions and helped develop analytical skills, but there comes a time when planned outlines become a paint-by-number exercise. Point D is determined; connect the dots beginning with A.

I keep a calendar of obligations: birthdays, doctors' appointments, that sort of thing. If I can remember to use the calendar and can find it, the future, when it becomes the present, is better organized and much calmer.

But planning your love life is not a paint-by-number exercise nor does it always follow a carefully crafted script. In fact, overplanning will destroy spontaneity, take the mystery out of adventure, eliminate the surprise in exploration. "Go with the flow" is sound advice (much better than "roll with the punches"). Your partner may determine the flow and it may not be according to your carefully orchestrated outline. Be flexible and patient. Above all, patient. To your loved one say, "I love you." All your plans begin with that. Your love is the strongest security you can offer. You and that person need each other. Hold tight, and with your holding, voice the words of bonding.

Your loved one may fear the bonding; the bond of love carries within it its own seed of possible disappointment, the loss of you.

He or she already has lost someone to death or divorce or separation and may view a new, intimate bond as a great risk. Bonding and loss are in the nature of opposites. Bonding risks loss although potential loss does not ensure bonding.

Except. Except that you need to bond with someone who understands your loss, who comforts you and loves you through the past. Together, that's the key word here, working through the past, leaving it behind, confronting and planning for the future. Together.

When paperback books first came to America from England, their covers were staid black printing on plain, dull, colored paper. Once they took hold, and especially once fiction was printed in paperback form, artists took over the cover designs. Inevitably, from snow-capped mountains to arid deserts to primeval forests, in canoes,

on shipboard, atop castle walls, facing hardened crimi-
nals, tribesmen, pirates, the covers portray a handsome
half-dressed male with one arm holding a weapon and
the other wrapped around a beautiful, full bosomed
woman in period costume, homespun or fur, her dress
ripped off one shoulder. Sometimes she holds a gun or a
knife or a spear. It is all erotically trite. The covers help
sell tens of thousands of books.

Over the years I have come to see the appeal of the
covers. It's not always the handsome hero or the overly
endowed heroine; often the appeal is the embracing arm
and the pair's "we'll face it together against all odds"
stance. Or so I rationalize. My rationalization is based on
reality. After a particularly horrific disaster, my morning
paper pictured a man and a woman who had lost everything. The woman was quoted as saying, "We're alive,
we're together, we'll survive."

They will do more than that. Together they will
reach into the depth of their love, and arm in arm, they
will prevail over their loss. Together they will accomplish
what neither could do alone. Love makes that potential a
reality. That couple faces a new day; what has happened
has happened; it is time to move on into the future. So
with you. Turn your back on the past, taking with you
only that which was good; jettison the bad; it serves no
purpose. Then, with your loved one by your side, face
the dawn of your new day and walk arm in arm, heart in
heart into the future.

In the nature of life, you will be walking toward your
sunset. In the procession of glorious days ahead, bask in

the sunlight the two of you are creating for yourselves. Who knows when the last sunset will be. You've just begun your new life. Rejoice in that and in the hope that your new life will be endless.

Age and the ever present possibility of separation can make love more meaningful; age and the potential for separation can make passionate love more real because we know "endless" to be a misguided hope. Yet, if we don't behave as though our love and partnership was forever, we are cheating ourselves and the one we love. It was Erasmus who wrote, "It is Folly alone that stays the fugue of Youth and bears off louring Old Age,"

If love be folly, then embrace it all the more. It will not reverse our seniority, but it will make you feel and behave younger and it does bear (hold) off looming old age. Love promises treasures of the heart that are intangible, treasures that are yet to be discovered—even in our senior years.

Reality Check

Are things what they are?
Is reality what is,
whatever that is,
hot flashes or seminal star?

Presumably, for a stretch of time, you've been having grand and wonderful senior moments. You've been focused on discovering, reaching out to and loving an incredible someone, getting your egos in tune, dealing with fears, planning your future.

We know, in real life, there are things that go bump in the night; seas are not always calm; winds may not be fair.

It's time for a reality check. Your love may not be the happy reality you dreamed.

I've dreaded writing this chapter, and in point of fact, it is the last chapter I wrote, placed here in the midst of happy progress because this is the time to really consider just what you and your loved one have—or haven't achieved.

In my ideal world it rains only at night; the sun shines brightly every day; the air is fresh smelling and clean; beach sand is pristine, lapped by gentle waves; wilderness is pure; the lamb does lie down with the lion; life is unsullied; and if there are problems, in the end love prevails and everyone lives happily after.

Fat chance!

Life is far more rough and tumble.

Somewhere along the heavenly highway to bliss, you have to come down out of the clouds to deal with what's real, because, when you are in love, on one level you're giving form and color and substance to an illusion, creating rainbows and building castles in the sky.

In that sense, your love and your emotional acts of loving are so singular and so personal they cannot be seen or touched, weighed or measured by anyone else, not even your intended partner. Loving is not a secret reality; people love and have a loved one, but your love is your internal secret no matter how often and how loudly you declare it. Love itself is not unique; it's your love that is unique.

Oh, yes, love is very real—and often an unrealizable illusion, illusion being another word for what you wish, your unfulfilled hopes and unrealized dreams, and in that meaning, not real, not yet anyway. Maybe not ever.

Hopes and dreams. I've said much about the future. In the biblical "Song of Songs," the singer tells us, "This is my beloved. This is my friend…" with whom the future will be spiritually completed in the days of love to come.

Future does not mean some vague distant time; it means now, today and tomorrow, what begins today and carries on through tomorrow and the days after tomorrow, forever.

One of the realities you may face is that your loved one does not see the future as immediate or beginning in the present now. Perhaps the most he/she offers is an indefinite maybe. You are ready to commit yourself to an endless life together; he/she is not.

So, pairing with the reality of your love is another reality: confusion. Where do you go from here?

That's when your love reality may become a dark reality. You think of love as the color white, the purest of the pure, untainted, yet a black shroud hangs forlornly over your heart. Your wonderful illusion is marred. You haven't been rejected; you've been put on hold; for the present you're a convenient fixture.

Perhaps your intended life partner simply is not ready for the ultimate commitment, fears and doubts not fully defeated and not having been banished to the past. Perhaps she/he is not sure her/his love is strong enough to risk unswerving union. Perhaps romantic love is not reciprocated.

An acquaintance said to me one day, "I'm having a tough time. 'Gerald' says he loves me, as a friend, I guess, but he doesn't want me to be in love with him. I can love him but I shouldn't be in love with him."

If that's true, that woman's romantic love never may be reciprocated. Her declining intended may believe honestly, to misuse the feminist slogan from 1980, a man without a woman is like a fish without a bicycle. In other words, a woman in his life is someone useless; he simply does not want a female partner, or at least not that woman.

Or a woman may enjoy a man's companionship from time to time yet reserve her intimate affection for her female friends. And a man, just as simply, may enjoy the occasional company of a woman but prefer the bachelor life with his buddies. Either, especially seniors, confronted with a gender choice, may choose their closest friends from among those of the same gender, often for the sole purpose of making life simpler and less complicated.

That aside, there is a difference between "I love you" and "I'm in love with you," subtle as it may seem. "Love me but don't be in love with me" is acceptance of one as a friend and rejection of that one as a lover. For the one addressed, it's being held onto and being held off at the same time.

The holding onto and holding off can be a sincere expression of affection and an honest, direct statement that romantic love is not going to be returned, what Bette Davis's character in the movie "Now Voyager" said, "Oh, Jerry, don't ask for the moon. We have the stars." Granted, that's not what Jerry wanted to hear when he wanted the moon.

Or holding onto/holding off can be a form of exploitation, using the expression of love—until, as my acquaintance feared, someone better comes along. "You can love me, but I'm really looking for Mr./Mrs. Right."

If you're the would-be lover, it's easy to be taken advantage of. Knowing you are may be worth it. There's always the possibility of one's dream coming true; besides, you really enjoy being with the one you love at whatever level he/she allows.

"Allows." That may be a love ending sword. I know a man who hoped to be allowed to be a part, even if a minor part, of his loved one's life. It never happened. He had asked to be; beyond that he believed he had no right to attempt to maintain the relationship, even as a friend; she, apparently, encouraged no contact, and as an old song said, he sat disappointed by an unringing telephone, her silence being the dreaded, final message.

Consider such statements as "Keep in touch" or "Let's be friends" or "It was nice to see you again." Often such declarations are polite ways of saying goodbye, a formal farewell which upon reflection had been forecast but not accepted. Such statements will tell you there is nothing left, nil, zilch, zero.

Or "I value your friendship," which undoubtedly translates more accurately into "I'll call you if I need something, otherwise...." There's an old, cynical proverb that states the exploitive potential: "When a friend is in need, then he makes much of his friendship." And to conclude this brief collection of relationship ending statements, there is the nefarious "Call me if you need anything; I'll help you—if I'm not busy." "Call me; I'll help" fulfills the need to be socially graceful, but the message is clear: don't ask. You're not even on his/her priority list. There's an old saying, "When you've read the last page, close the book's cover." In this regard, we might echo Pushkin's lines:

We need the wit that nature gave us
To face our foes as all men must,
But from the ones we love and trust,
From our good friends, may Heaven save us!

❦ ❦ ❦

A commitment to love and to cherish demands so very much. Rightfully so.

But sometimes the pledge of fidelity cannot be made nor can the promise to love but you alone.

My talk radio was on as I checked this manuscript for grammatical mistakes. Two women were talking about fidelity (or, more accurately, the lack of the need for it). I am familiar with some the poetry of one of the women speaking, so I was not surprised when one woman said that infidelity was okay because her partner (husband, mate?) wanted her to be happy. Thus if infidelity made her happy, it was okay. The other woman agreed. It was reminiscent of the best-selling book from decades ago, *Open Marriage*, which argued for infidelity.

By the time I gave them my full attention, they had moved on to other items. Did I hear what I thought I heard? Or did I think I heard the rationale used so often to excuse infidelity? I can't be positive.

Infidelity within a committed relationship and adultery within a marriage strike me as the worst forms of betrayal. In that belief perhaps I'm terribly old fashioned and outdated. The allegedly committed person who reports the number of casual acquaintances bedded severs all commitments and slanders all words of love. The individual who includes random lovemaking as one of life's "optional trips" denies respect to his/her partner. The partnership is dissolved whether he/she wants a partner to be happy or not.

I've heard the excuse often. "It didn't mean anything." Nonsense. In a recent TV show, a woman discovered her boyfriend making love to another woman. "But it was just sex," he explained. "I love you." Street pucks.

Lovemaking is too intimately personal to not mean something. For one partner, it's a minor trophy, one more notch of sexual accomplishment, one more proof of sensuality, one more prisoner taken. For the betrayed, it means rejection and worthlessness, not being good enough, convenient but second-rate. Love, if there is any, has become a devastating weapon of emotional abuse.

Here is one area where the distinction between a marriage partnership and a domestic partnership without marriage is evident. Infidelity within marriage is adultery, a breaking of spiritual and legal vows. It is one of the leading cause of divorce, often masquerading as "incompatibility" or emotional abuse in those states which allow such claims. There are legal ramifications in divorce settlements.

In a nonmarriage relationship, the aggrieved partner has few legal recourses. In an earlier age, the "injured" partner might have sued his or her partner's new sex mate for "alienation of affection," but today such a suit would be laughed out of court, if it got to court. The phrase "consenting adult" would apply, and if you were the one cheated on, it would be assumed you knew what you might confront and therefore consented to it. In other words, you accepted all risks and alone bear the consequences.

As with all things, there are exceptions. The rich and

famous, in 1979, gave us a new word, "palimony." By 1981 the word achieved legal standing: a former *pal* (not a spouse) was seeking *alimony*, and a few high profile lover's cases proved that one can get rich by suing the rich.

❦   ❦   ❦

A while ago a semi-retired psychologist, a widower, came to see me. "I heard you were writing a book about senior love," he began.

"Yes," I told him. "I've been working on it for a year."

"I was going to write such a book. Most of my clients now are seniors."

"Why don't you?"

"I got involved, emotionally, sexually. It wasn't working out. I became my own patient, so to speak. I lost all objectivity."

Since his wife died, the psychologist has maintained a modest practice, seeing clients a couple of days a week. Most of his work is in bereavement therapy and aging, the latter because children didn't know what to do with aging parents or because aging clients didn't know how to accommodate to their advanced years. And there are seniors who need help with issues of love and sex.

"But I haven't come to ask about your book. Just wish you luck." He paused. "Strange, isn't it. We listen and give guidance to others; then when we need someone to listen to us and perhaps direct us, we've no one to talk with. That's why I'm here. I need someone to listen."

He told me I could write up his predicament, reserving his right to review it. I agreed, if I decided to use his problem, but, I assured him, I was a good listener, and if he had a concern which I might help ease, that was the only agenda item.

"I love a woman. She does not love me. We had a few months of sweet passion but it didn't last." It was a familiar situation.

"Here's my immediate problem. She wants to date casually; says she likes me; you know the bit. I want to—and I don't want to. It's the don't want to part that troubles me. When we're together, no matter the conversation, I have an insatiable desire to hold her, to hug her, to touch her. It isn't going to happen; I know that.

"Yet that's my single thought. I don't mean that I have to have intercourse with her. I think I can manage to get along without that. I've come to think if she offered I'd refuse. I don't think I could do it with someone who didn't love me or at least have great affection for me. It probably would be like making love to a pillow. I need the feeling a tender touch can give."

I wanted to say get over it, and I wanted to say something about obsessions, but here was a professional who in our conversation proved he knew the answers. He just hadn't been able to apply them to himself.

My tactic was to listen mostly, ask an occasional question, reflect back what I heard, and hope that in so doing he would hear himself. He didn't expect answers; his primary need was to tell his pain to someone who would listen. His was, in effect, a plea, not so much for help as it was for understanding and sympathy.

We continued to meet while he worked through his rejection. Learning to unlove, if there is such a concept, or falling out of love is much harder than falling in love. It's not just falling out of love; it's giving up the love one has created and nurtured while managing to keep the heart intact.

It's not uncommon, although for seniors it seems more dramatic and traumatic. From my experience, I think seniors fall deeper in love and have a harder time of it when love fails. Some will say that's because seniors know they have few opportunities for love, but my thinking is that seniors, with all their years of experience, make a much greater emotional investment in love and therefore run a greater emotional risk, and with that they suffer more when a love affair doesn't work out.

Seniors generally seem to understand and appreciate what love demands, and most seniors are conscious of the efforts necessary to make a new love work. When love fails, they are defeated because they assume full blame for the failure.

❦ ❦ ❦

A warning: there are occasions when keeping your mouth shut is sound advice. Your reality check may reveal truths hard to acknowledge and harder still to accept. Your thoughts may run wild as you try to analyze the impediment to or the failure of your love to prevail. If you have failed and love is not reciprocated, you want to know why; that's natural, an inevitable consequence of disappointment.

Voicing your analysis may not be wise, especially if you are trying to interpret your would-be partner's conflicting and/or contradictory words and behavior.

For instance, your "would-be" seems affectionate when the two of you are alone; in a social setting you're ignored and/or demeaned. Or, in private you're granted a tentative hug; in public you're denied. Or, you venture a joint project or adventure idea; your "friend" follows through—with one of his/her friends.

Bite your tongue. You're confused and hurt. You are not number one. Your thoughts are negative thoughts. Giving voice to them will make things worse because you will be seen as demanding too much or failing to give space. Voicing your confusion may end any chance of righting the floundering ship of love.

I know this flies in the face of desirable communication, but believe me, this conversation will be one sided. You will dig a hole from which you cannot escape because drawing attention to mixed signals will put your friend on the defensive and he/she may retreat beyond your ability to maintain any meaningful contact.

♥ ♥ ♥

I was told once, "I'd like to date 'Roger.' But if I do, I'm spoiling my chances of meeting someone to marry." I understood the statement; she was hunting. Unfortunately, poor Roger didn't fulfill her requirements. And that was fair enough, too, except the person who spoke never quite let Roger go. She held on to him just tightly enough to give him a taste of encouragement, and Roger, deeply in love, continued to work through the steps of love, not coming to grips with the fact that he was being used and that his illusionary highway of love was a blind dead end.

Finally, Roger reached the point where he knew—like experiencing a gorgeous Indian summer day in the autumn of his life; it was all so unexpected and beautiful—it couldn't last.

"I've seen love's secret place and for a brief moment looked into its infinitely deep soul," he told me in words something like these, "and now I see only from a distance. I ask myself, what is better than having loved?"

I shook my head, waiting for him to continue. "Having someone's love; that is better. While you have it, you're not a loser, not yet anyway."

Is it better to have loved and lost than never to have loved at all? Most would say yes, weighing the joys of loving, transient as they might be, against never having experienced the high joys.

❦   ❦   ❦

Years ago, a charming couple came to my office. They were going to be married, the second time for each. Their request was simple. Could they join the group for married couples I had put together a year or so earlier?

Originally, the group was for couples undergoing stressful adjustments in their lives, from parenting to career changes, illness to internal conflicts, who, because of the stress, had lost most or all social contact with others. The couple about to be married were without social contacts.

The group had been an immediate success. The format was simple: meet in a couple's home for after dinner dessert, play a few mixer parlor games, sit in a circle, drink coffee (nothing stronger was served) and exchange concerns. What I wanted to happen happened: the awareness that people are not alone in their misery, the knowledge that difficulties can be shared, that stress strikes everyone, that people care, and that a social group setting sometimes can be a proper setting for dealing with certain problems.

More than because of my role, people did find sympathetic understanding and support. Several couples became close friends, and to my knowledge, every couple reentered the larger social mix from which they had thought they had to hide.

Later, long after the group was left on its own, the woman I mentioned asked to see me. She had a problem of a personal kind. She had fallen in love with a co-worker. Because her husband was working out of town, she and her new love had been able to spend a week together.

She had worked through the adultery part of it, she said. Her problem was, she realized she had not been in love with the other man. In fact, she still loved her husband, dull as he was.

"Well, say something," she demanded after telling her story.

"Right now I'm a listener," I told her.

"And you think I'll solve my own problem?"

"As a matter of fact, yes."

"With your nudging?"

"Maybe."

My point here is that we know the answers to most of our questions—if we can manage to ask the right questions. We know what's right and what's wrong; we know how we feel and even why we feel as we do; we have a genetic sense of behavior as well as a learned sense of proper conduct. I'm happy to report that the wife worked very hard at her marriage and that the harder she worked the more attentive and open to new adventures her husband became. Sometimes you do win one.

❦ ❦ ❦

Sometimes love blinds us. We need to step away from ourselves in order to see ourselves.

Take this example: you've worked so hard to prove yourself worthy of being loved there are times when being in love is not fun. You're "on stage" every moment; each day is a pass/fail test; you cannot relax and sit back and enjoy being in love because you're afraid of committing a love-threatening blunder or omitting a loving deed; fun eludes you.

There's an old Spanish proverb, "Whoever really loves you will make you cry." Well, sometimes someone who doesn't love you will make you cry. If the one you love creates that condition, then something is terribly wrong. Loving someone is serious stuff, no doubt about it; not having fun is a tragic blemish on the whole affair and may tell you all kind of things you don't want to know.

A reality check asks the question, "Does he/she really

want a full-time partnership?" John Dowland claimed, "What poor astronomers are they / who take woman's eyes for stars."

Do you see what's there in your loved one's eyes or do you see what you hope is there? Dowland's statement is proper for either gender. How do you know that what you see reflected back to you is fact and not just wishful fancy?

One answer is, you don't, but that's dodging the question. If you have taken the steps of love to this point, you rightfully deserve a response. Whether it's the response you want is moot. Forget for a minute what you hope will be the reply. Have you received any feedback?

Certainly you have, and some of it must have been positive, otherwise you wouldn't have come this far. The question then becomes, what are you really seeing and/ or hearing? What is your reality?

Put it another way: is your reality in tune with your loved one's reality? Don't guess; ask. Sit down and talk about individual wants and needs, find out where you stand, and above all, if he/she is worth it, be understanding and patient, with yourself as well as with him/her. Check your ego at the door; this is a time for mutual understanding, not for some kind of oneup(wo)manship.

❦ ❦ ❦

What is reality? Is there a substitute for love? Wealth may attract, social position may appeal, public power and acclaim may seduce, and some would take any or all instead of love. When Bernice Kanner, a columnist for

Bloomberg LP, the giant financial media company, did her online research for her two books, *Are You Normal* and *Are You Normal About Money,* she received as many as sixteen thousand (16,000) responses per question.

"Money has become the new sex," she says. Her questions reveal that ninety-two percent of Americans would rather be rich than find the love of their life. (Parenthetically it should be noted that her questions were addressed to the wealthiest members of society, those who had enough money to need financial investing services.)

I suppose I should understand (but I don't have to like) the money need of the ten percent of Americans who would "lend" their spouses to someone else for a night and the additional sixteen percent who would consider it; I'm not sure I understand (and I certainly don't like) the idea that twenty-five percent of Americans would, for enough money, become prostitutes. Or the one out of fourteen (seven percent) who would commit murder.

The once popular song, "Pennies from Heaven," doesn't stand a chance nowadays. Even allowing for inflation, dollars won't cut it. Thousands of dollars might, but they make for a lousy song.

Don't get me wrong; there is nothing wrong with money; I wish everyone not only had the money they need to live comfortable lives but had enough more to enjoy some of the pleasures only money can buy: vacation travel, secure retirement and/or the financial ability to contribute to worthy social causes.

But you might hug your bankbook and your stock portfolio; they won't hug back; they won't wipe your tears or shout your joys. They can give you power; they won't give you respect. That, along with love, is something you cannot buy. Someone might love your wealth; that someone will not love or respect you.

It has been suggested that in the matrix of love, money and material possessions should not matter. After all, you've never seen a hearse pulling a U-haul. But money often does matter—and, if Kanner's statistics are valid, love is in very short supply.

Authors James Redfield and Michael Murphy and counselor Sylvia Timbers in their *God and the Evolving Universe* argue just the opposite. (The title is a misnomer. God doesn't even make the index and there's nothing about an evolving universe.) "Evolution has brought...us to the brink of transformation...[for] our greater potential...[of practicing] the spiritual mysteries of existence," they say. Utopia is just around the corner; we humans will, via spirituality (the authors' word for love), finally rise above our animal instincts.

I doubt it. Right now spirituality (love) is lacking, and where it is found, it is ridiculed by a materialistic world population.

Does that mean love cannot prevail? Money, position and power seem poor lovers in the long run and none is as faithful and loving (although many people disagree with me on this) as a good man or woman. Perhaps I should capitulate and say a good rich man or a good wealthy woman. "For richer, for poorer" may be the key theme for many, with the emphasis on richer. You'll have to decide whether to evaluate your partner or whether you are being evaluated by your partner in terms of dollars or love.

❦   ❦   ❦

Another issue in any intense relationship, senior or not, is the issue of sex. If the expression of sexuality is not at the center of the relationship, it is not far off. That's an unavoidable consequence of the male/female relationship.

Two ideas about a sexual relationship are true. One: engaging in the ultimate sex act is one of, if not the most, fulfilling mutual physical expressions of love, and two: sexual activity can threaten a friendship.

Without asking the question, you know the answer: it is possible meaningfully and lovingly to physically hold someone, cuddle with someone, without engaging in the final act of lovemaking. A kiss, a hug, a held hand, a look can convey love in sublime ways and often can be more meaningful than sexual intercourse.

If your illusion is a long night of lovemaking and the reality is abstinence, it's time to check with your partner. How do you handle that? What's comfortable for you? For him/her? What can you agree on? What is mutually satisfying and fulfilling?

You can answer your questions for yourself; you cannot answer for your partner. That requires communication. If your partner says, "Don't be in love with me," he/she is saying no to a romantic relationship. That puts love on an entirely different level.

Back off. I don't mean to give up the whole idea of loving him/her; I mean back off, give your relationship space, give the one you love some breathing room. And amid the disappointment, give yourself some breathing room too, because now you are confronted with a whole new dimension, and the question becomes, can you maintain a close, loving (but not being in love with) friendship?

If you are facing that choice, the disappointment will be great. Your romantic illusions will be shattered. There is no comfort in acknowledging the risk you assumed. If there is any comfort, it will come in time, perhaps in time to recover your sense of balance.

Mending a broken heart takes time. There's no shame in saying, "For a moment there was happiness, and that happiness was you." Whether you believe it or not, the world understands. You are not the first disappointed lover nor will you be the last, just unique because it's your heart that aches.

Nothing in the world prohibits you from loving someone, hopeless as that may be, even if that someone doesn't want your love. Walk away. In the long run you'll do yourself a favor. If your love is genuine, you will not force yourself upon another. You will love that person enough to withdraw, allowing him/her the freedom you would demand for yourself. It will be difficult, but you will know you loved strongly and sincerely enough to do the *right* thing.

That small, selfless act may ease some of the disappointment and frustration. Only you will know the painful courage it took, but you will know. And there is much to be said for the selfless, loving act.

However brief the flame,
remember the light,
and thank the stars
that for a moment
joy filled your life.

❦   ❦   ❦

The analogy may seem insensitive and as cold as an icy shower. Your reality check is similar to having your old, rickety automobile inspected and repaired. You're got some miles on you. Loving has been like a new paint job and new tires and a new battery. The old car is spiffed up and ready to go.

The question is not can it go but will it go? And here the analogy fails somewhat. The fuel that drives you is your love for someone. Without that, you can manage to get to the corner store; you aren't going to the flowered garden of your dreams.

If you and your partner are not a couple, and friends are not considered a couple, the word *partner* is inappropriate. You have a friend, but in no way will that friend want the *couple* word used. In fact, he/she will go out of his or her way to prove to the world you are not a twosome. You must prepare yourself for that, another negative aspect of reality.

Indeed, your reality check may not sustain your hopes or reinforce your dreams or encourage your moonstruck ego.

On the other hand, a reality check acknowledges how far you have come and tells you something about where you are. It is a review and a preview of what might be in store for you and for your beloved.

If you pass your self-imposed reality check, the next step has to do with committing, as in pledging your love for the rest of your lives. A commitment should be based on mutual understanding, trust, a sense of security, and a hope that is fearless. Committing is not to be taken lightly. If the steps you have taken are not sound or adequate, now is the time to find out, before you make a commitment on inadequate foundations or accept a commitment not reinforced with certainty.

Or perhaps there is no next step. You've come as far as the focus of your love allows. What then? A sense of loss, of disappointment, of defeat? You went through that once; you can get through it again. Life will not be the same. Comfort will be difficult to attain. You tried; for a while you made someone happy; you were happy. Now, in Lily Tomlin's words, "We're all in this alone."

Committing

Pledge to life. Stand naked
of pretense in your love
as in your lovemaking.
Love is life untainted.

You've made your reality check, a gloomy but necessary business. I hope you passed unscathed—and wiser. Now it's on to happier steps.

If a word needs defining or explaining, it might not be smart to use it. *Commit* is a word of various meanings from "appoint" to "yield."

But *commit*, the verb (and *commitment,* the noun) contains so much of what has been said, it is the correct word. Entrust, pledge, confide, give, assure, choose, and a dozen more synonyms are meaningful and to the point.

You have chosen and reached out to someone; you have given your heart to that someone; you have assured that person of your love; you have confided your fears and have been entrusted with his/hers. From the fifteenth century song, "The Nut-Brown Maid," you sing to your beloved, "For in my mind, / of all mankind I love but you alone."

If you haven't already, now is the time to pledge not only your love but your commitment to the future.

This is the final step in securing your love's response; the remaining steps are learning to appreciate the rewards of having a loving partner and savoring in anticipation the intimate partnership promised.

You've said "I love you" a million times; you've shown your intentions with dozens of red and yellow, pink and orange roses; you've shared scores of projects and adventures; you've spent countless hours on the telephone; you may have composed volumes of love poetry—all intended to demonstrate your love; you've showered him/her with gifts from faraway places; you've cooked a trillion meals; you've done a zillion chores; you've looked longing into his/her eyes—all intended to demonstrate your love.

Have you voiced the ultimate commitment?

For some that voicing is the risky, "Will you marry me?"

For others it's the risky, "Will you be mine, without marriage?"

Right off you say, "But marriage is the goal, isn't it?"

And the answer is a tentative, "Yes—and no."

The goal of receiving "yes" to a marriage proposal needs no explanation, and the risk of rejection is self-evident. So let's back up. You find someone you love, you declare your love, you are loved in return, and a mutual love is affirmed. Oh, love! The strength of it, the faith of it, the illusions and dreams of it! The future enwrapped in love! Praise the future!

But, said the 1922 Nobel Prize physicist Niels Bohr, "Predictions are hard, especially about the future." That insightful line applies to the future of everything in life.

Your suggestion of marriage is turned down. What

happened? What went wrong? Maybe nothing went wrong. Perhaps you asked the wrong question or offered the wrong milieu at the wrong time.

It was Goethe who said, "Love is an ideal thing, marriage a real thing; a confusion of the real with the ideal never goes unpunished." That jaundiced view cannot go unnoticed; there are "real things" that can discolor the ideal.

One reason for refusal that deserves mention may be as mundane (which does not make it less convincing) as one's estate, the inheritance one plans to leave to children and grandchildren (and/or to charity, siblings, or others). While there are prenuptial safeguards, that is, legally drawn "what's yours is yours, what's mine is mine" agreements, many seniors simply don't want to risk the slightest potential for a fiscal mistake. Nor do they dare chance the possibility of a partner's long term illness and care eating up both partners' resources.

It is not an insignificant concern. It does not mean one's love is less or that love is overshadowed by crass materialism. It may be the honorable need to "keep the money in the family." A new domestic partner, however loved and respected, is not "in the family" as are children and grandchildren.

For most of us, we're not talking millions and millions of dollars; wish that we were. For most of us, we're talking about far smaller amounts and items of family interest other than dollars.

"Don't sweat the small stuff" is good advice. However, in establishing a new partnership, there is no small stuff. If differences or disagreements arise, most often they arise over the small stuff that has become big stuff. Money matters, no matter the amount, is never small stuff.

And it's possible, of course, that a financial excuse is just a cop-out burying other fears or evading other doubts.

❦ ❦ ❦

I can't guess the many reasons for refusing marriage. I hint at a few and solve none of your frustrations. Back up a bit and consider a different question.

Maybe the question is not about marriage but is about fidelity. Does he or she "love but you alone?" We've discussed some of that already.

For the moment forget marriage. A commitment can be made without wedding vows. For many seniors that's a necessary condition to a commitment. It leaves space. (It also leaves room to back out, but more of that later.) It promises freedom.

What follows is a condensation of conversations. A woman said, "I like coupling; I don't want to be a couple." I made no response. After a time she said, "I like to travel, I love great food, I enjoy good sex." I shrugged my shoulders. "Marriage is a trap; as soon as I got married, I wanted out."

Now I could ask why.

"He wanted me to take care of him."

"He was ill?"

"No. I had to earn money; I had to cook; I had to clean house. Then he became ill, and I had to take care of him.

"It's a trap. Don't you see? He became sick. I had to take care of him. If I marry again, he'll become sick; I'll become sick. Who will take care of me? I'll grow old and be sick."

And there she stated the real problem: she was afraid of growing old. The travel she loved, the food she enjoyed, the sex she sought had become, unlike the exotic adventures of an earlier time, her way of dealing with the fact of aging; they "proved" her eternal youthfulness. Or to state the fact in another way, it was her way to stall, postpone, or evade the inevitable: one last mile, one last conquest, one last cigarette, one last meal before the final onslaught of old age. To make a commitment to a relationship was, in her mind, giving in to old age, an ironic emotional gymnastic twist, associating marriage with being old.

There is no way to turn back the biological clock. Aging happens; it's as inevitable as, well, dying. Denial works for a while, but sooner or later the inevitable future becomes one's reality. This woman will face hers alone, the untouchable faces on television her only company. It's likely her memories will be of episodes only, little flashes of pleasure moments, none of happiness, surely none of love.

❦ ❦ ❦

I would counsel one to consider carefully the fear factor. You may not have a fear of being old or tied down or closed in; such fears can be very real to one who does, and they can be determining factors in deciding the depth of commitment one makes.

As for marriage, I dislike the phrase *tying the knot* and the word *wedlock*. To me, "tying the knot" and "wedlock" sound like a medieval prison sentence. At best, tying the knot evokes images of a short leash. Both, the knot tied and the lock slammed shut upon being wed, imply human captivity and ownership of another human being.

Here a particular observation about space in a romantic relationship. Sometimes there is a conflict between the need for intimacy and the need for identity.

Enlarging one's ego circle to include or to be included in another's does not mean losing one's own identity or having one's identity swallowed up by another or denying the individuality of another. Always, each partner must be regarded by the other as an individual of worth and of integrity.

A woman told me once, "He wants me to be him." I hoped that was not so. Men complain often that "She's trying to remake me." In her image? Again, I hope that is not true. What one wants for the loved one is that he or she will grow in individual strength and fulfillment because of the partnership.

The worry that's often present, of course, is that by giving oneself to another one gives away one's individuality, one's integrity, that in an intimate, loving relationship one gives up one's own life in favor of another's. That should not be the case.

A commitment, whether a formal marriage or a self-proclaimed partnership, that does not provide space in which each can blossom and grow is not a commitment to an equal partnership but rather is a denial of equality. How one's space is used is another matter, but each partner must be assured of space and encouraged to use it.

Again, as with so much we've said, honest and sincere communication is a must. If you and your loved one are not on the same wavelength, trouble is brewing.

Definitions of "commit" are to surrender to, submit to, yield to, be tied to. And definitions of "pledge" are to press, compel, require, bind, or tie down. Let none of those meanings prevail. In seeking commitment, never press your wishes upon your partner or compel or require that person to behave in any way contrary to his or her own wishes.

And do not submit or yield or surrender to any suggestion that diminishes your integrity.

Nothing in a commitment to love and honor your beloved makes demanding or giving in to demands reasonable. It is not even rational.

You are committing to sharing; you are committing to equality; you are committing to partnership. You are not committing to servitude. Responsibilities are shared; there will be divisions of labor that are agreed upon, not demanded. Anything short of mutuality is destructive; love will be tainted by any suggestion of *me-ism* or superiority.

In a sound partnership, each contributes his or her skills and knowledge; each works hard to assist and support the other; both strive to make the partnership a true partnership. That's what love does; it strengthens each so that together both can achieve their full potential as individuals. In a truly creative love story, each partner achieves more than either could achieve being single and apart.

And only then will love have prevailed untainted.

❦   ❦   ❦

If marriage is not an option, should you live together? That's a decision only the two of you can make. If you've dealt with the ethical issues, if you've agreed on the social issues, if you are secure and comfortable making such an arrangement, there's no reason why you shouldn't. Provided—there's always a provision—you have committed to being a couple.

One of the fallouts of that commitment is that it says to the world-at-large, "Hands off. We may not be married in the eyes of the law, but we have become a pair in every other way."

"In the eyes of the law...." When you're a senior, the law doesn't much care. Pay your taxes, stay out of trouble, support good causes, and the law couldn't care less.

"In the eyes of God" may be something else, however. To commit and to live as a pair is, in the words of Genesis, going forth and multiplying (although that seems unlikely at an advanced age), but these words may cause great concern, for example, about sin and punishment. The Bible also says no one should lie with anyone other than husband or wife. If you are single, you aren't committing adultery, you aren't harming anyone physically or emotionally, there is no "injured" husband or wife, you are consenting adults, etc., etc. But....

Throughout history throughout the world, "family

relationships" outside of marriage (husband/wife) have been recognized if not tolerated. Some of the historical data as well as much of the current psychological and sociological evidence supports the present reality that the official marriage of a man and a woman is out of touch with people's lives. Please read these lines carefully; make sure you understand what I am saying.

In the United States year 2000 census, only 52 percent of our households were occupied by married couples. The number of unmarried couples living together in year 2000 increased by 72 percent over year 1990. American family structures are remarkably diverse and complicated.

Attorney Bill Mauk, helping hundreds of survivors of the September 11, 2001, terrorist attack on the Twin Towers in New York City, told the Associated Press, on February 17, 2002, "The stereotype of a traditional family (based on three thousand 9/11 survivors)...is probably the exception rather than the rule.... The law, to a significant degree, has not kept pace with the changing family."

Statistical data doesn't make something right or wrong.

"Norms" are what is at any given time. There are legions of questions to be answered by anyone, not just seniors, before becoming a cohabiting couple. And that's the point here, not the fact that others are doing it: *communication*, serious communication, and shared decision making is the point.

I support whatever decision you and your loved one make, but for heaven's sake, make it a joint decision after you have weighed all the issues and feelings. You are enjoying yourselves, and that alone may produce guilt. The test is, what is spiritually, emotionally, socially, and physically comfortable for you and your partner? The formal civil act of marriage may not be; anything other than that might be. They are your lives; live them as creatively and as full as you can—without injuring the spiritual and emotional health of your partner or yourself.

❦ ❦ ❦

Although I have announced previously the sexual orientation of this author and this book, I intrude here with a thought about homosexual partnerships because, while not the norm, they are a fact of life and because, as I mentioned in the opening, a mental health worker who read an early draft of this book raised the question of same sex partnerships and because, subsequently, another reader raised the same question.

I have been fortunate to have known many gays and lesbians, and count a handful among my most meaningful and influential role models, men and women who lived saintly lives and who contributed only goodness to my life.

No moral judgment is offered. That a woman can love another woman or a man another man is a historical as well as a contemporary social fact. In ancient Sparta, for instance, it was expected that both females and males would engage in same sex relationships, that in spite of the idea that the ideal Spartan was soldierly, stoical and indifferent to both pleasure and pain. A massive 1951 study of 190 societies throughout the world (see *Columbia Encyclopedia*, 5th edition) revealed that approximately 70 percent considered homosexual behavior acceptable. That number did not include the so-called Western cultures.

Homosexuality is not learned nor is it in the genes. Theories for its existence abound; none explain. Homophobia (fear of homosexuals) is one of our Western diseases. That society is beginning to recognize, understand, and tolerate the existence of homosexual love is a gigantic step toward human equality and the pursuit of happiness. While some American states have penalties for homosexual acts, the more enlightened guarantee "gay rights," including the right of gay and lesbian couples to adopt a child, and some states are formulating policies and languages to accommodate gay marriages.

I am one of those who would like to find a meaningful synonym for the word "marriage." That word has its roots in the earliest of human languages and means the union of two (or more, that is, plural marriage) people of different genders, but I understand the need expressed often by gays and lesbians for a formal civil and/or religious ceremony of union and for society's recognition of the same.

What I want to emphasize here, gender not withstanding, is that love has its requirements and its responsibilities. I don't care who you love. If you love another, you must continue to prove it. If you accept another's love, you must continue to earn it. It's as simple as that. And as strenuous.

Society has paid far more attention and given greater condemnation to gay love than lesbian love. It is hard to say why, and again the number of theories are legion. Neither the reasons for homosexuality nor its consequences are within the scope of this book other than to recognize its presence (and when homosexual love is genuine, its difficulties for the couple).

♥ ♥ ♥

However you define and work out your relationship, let there be no pretense, either between you and your partner or between you as a couple and society. Hiding, avoiding detection, pretending not to be what you are (a couple, heterosexual or homosexual), serves no worthwhile purpose and may cause more discomfort than simply letting the world discover your relationship and make of it what it will.

The "naked" reference at the opening of the chapter is simply this: unclothed, it's hard to conceal your warts and wrinkles and age spots. You have nothing behind which to hide, nor should you. I doubt a lover sees such signs, seeing only the whole of you and seeing you through love blessed eyes.

So with your friends and neighbors and children. They will see what you are, two people in love. There is no reason to hide that fact, no sense to pretend otherwise. If anything, most will be envious and wish their unions were as loving and as full.

♥ ♥ ♥

The essence of this chapter is to pledge yourselves to life and to commit yourselves to each other. Pledging to life is just that: as a couple to seek out and to find every joy, every pleasure, every measure of happiness you can. Committing to one another is the emotional environment in which joy, pleasure and happiness are found.

But more, committing is sharing the pains and sorrows life visits upon us; committing is understanding and support; committing is proving your love by loving.

❦ ❦ ❦

Over the years, my witnessing experience has been that the strongest unions have not been created by those who are so alike as to be emotional clones but by those of marked differences. People are not mere magnets, like attracting like, unlikes repelling.

We have our own magnetic fields which defy physics. One of the reasons two unalike people succeed in partnership is that each brings his/her own views, experiences and expectations to the union. Each enlarges the other's world, and in this instance one and one does not add up to two; one and one adds up to three and six and twenty and more. Each grows in wisdom and in strength. The differences are not noted and buried; the differences are noted and explored and become strengths from which mutual understanding and appreciation are created.

Earlier I extolled the picture of two lovers standing on the ramparts daring the world to conquer them. I believe that love creates that stance. But more, I believe that love motivates two people not only to defend themselves and each other against life's vicissitudes but urges them to explore a world not yet seen.

Two alike people may enjoy the same food, the same TV programs, the same bright colors and sweet smells of comfortable living, holding hands as they sit on the front porch watching the world pass by. A good, sound, solid life, sometimes to be envied.

Two people with dissimilar interests and tastes may help each other see new, different colors and smell new, fresh flowers. Instead of being spectators, they will have adventures of their own making. They will be part of the passing parade, marching to the combined beats of two hearts, following the road of life wherever it leads.

Seniors know, if they know anything, that the good life does not come to one's door; one must go in search of it. When you commit to another, promise to be a searcher; if you know something, teach it; if you feel something, express it; if you see something, share it.

I can't think of any higher aspiration than to be in a partnership with an adventurer who loves me or anything more exciting than to open new doors and to explore life with that person.

Sharing/Relaxing

Each is of the other,
giving to, taking from.
As entwined strands strengthen
the cord, trust each other.

In love, no power play
intrudes, no guard gates are
erected. Trust excludes
wars and threats of doomsday.

Nothing proves love more than sharing with your loved one all that life presents and offers, and no reward is greater than having someone with whom to share.

Thomas Moore got it exactly right: "Paradise itself were dim / and joyless, if not shared with him!" Or her! Here we reaffirm the joy of sharing without which every other facet of love, including intimacy, is hollow—even false. When defining love, I have emphasized sharing, togetherness, mutuality. Use whatever word you want. When you say "I love you," it means "I want to share life with you as my friend, my partner and my lover."

"I love you" does not mean "Let's get together and do what I want." Nor does it mean "I'll do anything you want."

So, what do we share? The quick answer is everything: hopes, dreams, joys, sorrows, good times, bad times. It means doing the dishes and taking out the garbage, raking the lawn, planning a trip or a party. It means comforting when illness or sorrow intrudes. It means managing the income and expenses. It means agreeing to disagree and to settle disagreements without rancor or bitterness.

It means supporting the other's projects, cheering successes and being sympathetic with failures. It means encouraging the one loved to tackle new ideas and then to learn along with him/her.

The list of opportunities to share is endless. Summarized, it adds up to "We're in this together and I'll do everything in my power not to let you down."

As important, sharing means sharing space, emotional as well as physical. Of the couple, each individual must have space to test her/his wings and to fly.

If we share life, we share the individual need to explore our own interests. Being in love does not mean we are clones; we do and will have individual and separate interests. If we really care about our partner, we will encourage him/her to follow those interests—even if he or she sometimes does so without our participation.

It was Grant Wood's *N by E* that opened with a story about a couple bored with life. One day the husband announced he was going to build a boat and sail to the South Seas.

"No, you aren't!" his wife shouted. He didn't; he didn't even build a rowboat; the only wild dream he ever had was dumped on.

The only thing Wood's two people shared was the

failure to confront life. Both watched life slip by, and when, finally, one wanted to engage in an adventure, any adventure, the other couldn't even share that impulse.

The need may not be to build a boat. Maybe it's taking an art course and painting masterpieces or learning to play the piano or harpsichord or reading all two dozen volumes of an encyclopedia or simply spending time with old friends in another country. Maybe it's a back country camping trip or the wish to stand in the Forbidden City or to float the Colorado River. Maybe it's a new wardrobe or new kitchen cabinets or a visit to children.

What's your loved one's aspiration? If you have to look for the answer, you're hopeless; you haven't been paying attention.

Sharing and giving space works two ways. You encourage, and in return you are encouraged, and the results, chopsticks or a smudged canvas or a bit of gossip or a canoe or pictures of a grand foreign experience are shared.

Obviously there are extremes in the way space is used. The "I'm going to rob a bank today" adventures of a Bonnie or a Clyde is beyond bounds. "I'm going to spend the next ten years in the mountains with the new high priest of yak milk living" also qualifies as stretching the relationship. But "I'd like to be part of that dig in Chile" may not be nor may the "I've been invited to sail the Halifax–Burmuda race."

There are legions of opportunities in which an

individual might test his/her wings and fly. Other things (money and health, for instance) being favorable, love encourages the adventure—and the adventurer.

If you worry that "flying" could mean your loved one might not return to the nest, you'd better back way down and figure out just what you mean by love and what love means to your partner. If love is not strong enough to allow each to sample new experiences, your love affair is in serious trouble.

Sharing, anyway you define it, does not mean tying up or tying down. Not everything has to be done together. What has to be shared, even if vicariously by one, is the joy for the adventure, its success and the fulfillment of the adventure taker.

Just as making room within your ego circle enlarges your circle, so giving space can bring you closer together.

Freedom within the loving relationship offers the couple one other tangible reward; it makes all those things done together that much sweeter. Remember, love is *not* two people through some misguided alchemy of emotional stewing becoming one, indistinguishable and unidentifiable. Love is the entwined strands of yarn that make the thread strong, the enwrapped small vines that gave Tarzan and Jane the ropes that carried them through the jungle, the woven fibers that make the hawsers that hold ships against the storms.

We entwine our limbs when making love. It is grand—it is not enough!

Our souls, if you like that word, must be wrapped

around the other's, embracing the other's, his/hers wrapped around ours. That is loving. But no matter how closely wrapped, remember that each strand is and must be an individual fiber of integrity and independence.

That is trust.

Giving your soul into the keeping of another is the ultimate test of love. "Into your hands, I give my keeping" is the most sublime and profound witness to loving trust I can imagine. It is love's completeness: spiritual, holy, as divine as anything here on earth can be.

It is said that those who cultivate gardens live longer and those who cultivate beautiful things are rewarded with vigor and appreciation, and in that sense, all lovers are gardeners, tenderly caring for their Eden.

❦   ❦   ❦

Sharing and caring rhyme, and when considering senior partnerships there may be a lot of necessary caring, since illnesses and injuries are likely to visit the elderly with some regularity. There is the potential for one partner becoming a caregiver, a nurse even, and that potential has to be considered. "In sickness and in health...." The sickness part is very real.

To love someone means to take care for him/her. My experiences suggest that the greater emotional pain is with the one who is sick; he/she does not want to be a burden, cause discomfort, need care. My experiences suggest, also, that the caregiver seldom thinks in terms of being burdened. The care given is given almost unconsciously, a loving gift to the one loved.

Young lovers never think of illness; that's an elder's

worry. And when elders are in love, usually they don't discuss their aches and pains; certainly they don't discuss impending ill health and prolonged sickness.

They should because they are prone to illness and disease. It's not a case of if; it's a case of when. When we were young, our life expectancy was for sixty or seventy more years; now it's for twelve or fifteen years, perhaps less, and the chance of one or the other partner suffering from cancer or cardiac problems or other life threatening illnesses means....

What does it mean? For one thing, it means that the rest of one's life and that of one's lover is compressed into a handful of years. Part of sharing is recognizing that fact and wringing from the remaining years all the happiness two people can.

For another thing, it means being prepared for the stress an illness can produce. It may be you went through that once; you might again. It will be no easier the second time. It may be harder. There's no way to forecast what's going to happen, but there are considerations to be discussed, and the better prepared you are, the easier it will be on each.

❦ ❦ ❦

There is a widespread impulse these days to rely on supernatural or otherworldly forces, utilizing fortune tellers and planet gazers to direct our lives, allowing them to make life's largest decisions for us. My daily newspaper offers forecasts and guidance; the "Old Farmers' Almanac" does likewise; "readers" of palms, bones and cards are within easy reach of my residence.

Should you depend on astrological forecasts or tarot cards or palm readings to determine your life? I don't believe so. If you ever do share your life, it should be because sharing is in your heart not in the stars, and because sharing is the rock solid foundation of love.

I'll give the last word on sharing to Rainer Maria Rilke. "Love consists in this, that two solitudes protect and touch and greet each other."

Greet, touch, protect. If you can keep the greeting forever new, the touch perpetually fresh, the protection eternally sure, you shall be entwined forever.

❦ ❦ ❦

If I can end the *Sharing* part with a quotation, I can introduce you to *Relaxing* with another quotation, this from Dorothy Sayer. "The worst sin—perhaps the only sin—passion can commit is to be joyless."

Relaxing in the context of seniors in love is very specific, as in letting down, dropping defenses and defensiveness, foregoing power plays and displaying ego. You hope the one you love does the same, and if both of you do, then you can begin learning the joy of being in love. Sayer is correct; passion must be joyful, has to be joyful, if love is to be valid.

Love without passion is an inhospitable desert; nothing will grow in a dry, bleak, arid relationship; love words will be as dust, touches will be as unforgiving stone—and love, if it blooms at all, will die quickly.

And how does one find the joy in passion? By relaxing. If that seems as though we're dancing round with the words, let's go on a bit.

When we drop our defenses, our shields, let our loved one see us for what we are without pretense or brag; when we are natural, off-stage, comfortable with our loved one; when we are secure in our love and secure in love's return; when we can lighten up, hang loose, tarry, be cool, be at ease, be at peace with ourselves, then we are relaxed.

Then love becomes fun.

If I've said it before, let me repeat it: to be understood is to be accepted; to understand is to accept.

Accepted, we no longer have to struggle for our place in our loved one's love light. We can enjoy the light for what it is: togetherness, shared hopes, friendship, partnership.

Relaxing does not mean sitting back, goofing off, letting the needs of love float away on the wind of "Gee, I've arrived." You have arrived, finally, but you've arrived at that place in the love process where a sense of being loved, the security of being loved, the knowledge of mutual love lets you take off your shoes and run gleefully with your mate through the remaining years of your lives.

Relaxing demonstrates the confidence of your love and the faith you have in your partner's love. Confidence and faith are joy, and joy is expressed in passion, just as passion is expressed by wild whoops and exuberant expressions of love.

When you are relaxed you are free, free to embrace your love with unrestrained enthusiasm, free from worry and doubt, free from inhibitions and conventions. You are free to invent new words and new ways of saying "I love you." You are released from the old world into a new world. And in your new world the word is *Joy*.

❦   ❦   ❦

"Your new world." We seniors live in a world far different from the world in which we were born and far removed from the world in which our parents loved and arranged "unions." We're well aware of the mechanical inventions and the medical advances that have taken place during our lives; we may not be as acutely aware of the social changes that have taken place even though we have been part of those changes. Specifically, I refer to changes within family structures and to the changing role of women.

Prior to World War II, the traditional woman's role in marriage (and in those partnerships without the formality of marriage) was to provide domestic services and sexual companionship, a role grounded in thousands of years of human history.

Women obtained voting rights after World War I (and exercised their power by demanding prohibition), but it was the Second World War that gave women a temporary status as their males' equal. Men went to war and women went into the factories and did men's jobs, often better than the men had done them. And women entered the armed services, sometimes as pilots doing dangerous and strenuous work or as front line nurses serving under fire.

However, when the war was concluded, all that was ignored as an aberration. Women returned to the kitchen and the bedroom. The result? The world's most gigantic baby boom and the reinforced ideal family concept of a husband as the bread winner and the wife as cook and nursemaid.

All those babies had other ideas. Rock music, a sexual revolution, social   revolutions shook the western world. It was the Age of Aquarius, the first sign of the zodiac in the western calendar, the dawning of a new age, the Aquarius symbol that looks like a squiggly equal mark.

In our generation, the dramatic family structure changes took place within eight or ten years. One day my children were watching June and Ward Cleaver bringing up the Beaver; the next day they were off to Woodstock; one day they were watching Davy Crockett defending the Alamo; the next day they were standing naked on stage in "Hair." The Cleavers' sterile world was replaced with free love, moon children, Woodstock, Idaho compounds—and later the highest divorce rate we have ever known. The highest teenage pregnancy rate also.

The negatives, however, are not the point to be debated here. Our children and grandchildren had transformed the traditional family. Seventy-five percent of women in a two-parent home work outside the home. Often the male is not the major bread winner; in 2002, about 30 percent (ten and a half million) female partners earned more than their mates. That's twice the rate of 1982. Women successfully balance motherhood and careers; many men are the stay-at-home child caregiver.

Women have achieved significant roles in every area, professional and otherwise. As Randi Minetor wrote in her *Breadwinner Wives and the Men They Marry*, "These women don't want power. They want an equal partner who shares everything, including chores."

The Cleavers in *Leave it to Beaver* were never real. Ward dressed for work but never seemed to; the family was white upper class, judging from the home and the presence of a maid; the biggest problem it faced was homework; June never took off her apron (and never got near the kitchen), a symbol of woman's role; Ward and June never expressed love, their marriage robotic and without affection; they never argued because they never disagreed; the whole sweet family was one sterile mass, the final make-believe attempt to preserve a family ideal that had gone the way of the dodo.

Within a decade many social conservatives wished it back because what became the alternative was too open and commitment free. When love is free, it is cheap—in more ways than one. Fortunately for society (to say nothing about the seventy-six million individual baby boomers, half of whom are about to enter the Social Security pay out system), there were second thoughts. Youth had its revolution; in many ways it was necessary whether we liked it or not; they modified male/female roles; the divorce rate now is going down; there's stability in more families (statistically, even if it's not immediately evident); partnerships (including marriage) on the whole are stronger.

Today the husband/wife (or however the partnership

is established) roles are dramatically different than when we were born. Women have not achieved full equality (under the law, maybe, but not yet culturally). Family roles have changed dramatically to the point where a man/woman partnership is coming to mean just that, a full partnership, not the earlier concept of the man as genetically (and reinforced by theology) superior to the woman.

For a couple of years, the dealership where I have my automobile serviced has had a female chief mechanic. The only question is, does she know her job? And the answer is an unqualified yes. Unfortunately, some males asked other, insensitive questions and refuse to have their vehicles evaluated by a women. I suppose they treat their girlfriends and wives with the same prejudice, demeaning their women and missing out on the rewards of a truly rewarding union of equals.

I recited these few illustrations because fulfilling the concept of meaningful sharing is impossible unless the one with whom you share is considered an equal.

Nothing in the immediate future is going to change our biological roles; for each of us, however, it's important to grasp the full meaning of equality within the relationship. *Our* and *we* become the most important pronouns we can speak. Spoken from the heart, they are love words.

If, and a big if it is, yours is a relationship of equals, and if there is no contest of egos, and if your partner's welfare is your primary concern, you can relax and enjoy one another because you know that the one you love loves you as an indispensable equal partner. What joy!

❦   ❦   ❦

There is one other component of relaxing demanding recognition. The couple has discovered love, has expressed it and has made a commitment, one partner to the other. The two behave as a couple; a sense of well being and elation surrounds and supports them. Then the purely physical enchantment fades and the intensity of the romantic aspect of the partnership lessens.

Is the partnership failing? Certainly not. The reality is that passion and infatuation, physical desire and intense concentration on mutuality cannot continue at the initial pace, as exciting and as "hot" as they were in the beginning.

If you understand the steps of love, you know the initial sexual excitement is not the adhesive holding everything together. You know that what holds a loving partnership together is being together, sharing interests and adventures, discovering not only each other but the new world your partnership has created.

You know that basic to everything is communication. If the *I* and the *me* and the *my* have been put to rest, in their place *we* and *us* and *our* will prevail. The therapist Michele Weiner-Davis recommends we practice "the Three T's: Time together, Talk, Touch." It is good advice.

All three activities bind and entwine us with our loved one and grant us the ability to deal with problems as they arise. Talking—and listening—are foundations upon which mutuality is built. You and your partner are in this life together, and that means not only doing things together but together dealing with each other's needs—emotional, spiritual, and physical.

In Tai Chi, there is an exercise called "Push Hands." Partners face one another with both hands lightly touching palms. The partners move their hands and arms in circular motions while simultaneously increasing or decreasing the hand pressure, as in giving or receiving.

The exercise is two fold: to maintain touch with your partner and to feel that touch strengthening and waning as the body gives and receives, the yin/yang of a partnership. In theory, equal pressure might be desirable, but life is give and take; emotions, like the tides, flow and ebb. The Push Hands exercise helps one sense the in/out, up/down, give/receive, light/dark, yin/yang of one's partner, hands pushing being the physical manifestation of the partners' hearts and minds. Life is give *and* take.

What is sought is harmony within the inevitable physical and emotional movements of each partner, each so in touch with the other that no matter what, touch is not lost.

One basic love need is touching and being touched, physically and emotionally. And that runs the entire gamut from sharing tearful moments of distress to sharing a fulfilling sex life. A gentle hand, a tender kiss, a soothing hug—whatever is needed to express empathy. A passionate embrace, a longing kiss, a loving placement of hands and feet—whatever enraptures you and him/her. The touch conveys the physical oneness of the relationship; the touch transmits the feelings of the heart.

Two hearts in harmony, synchronized, beating in rhythm, against all the ups and downs which may appear, can relax in each other's presence because they know how soundly and securely they are connected.

Healing

When hurting, the embrace:
the voiceless touch speaks words
from angels' songs. Doubt and fears
disappear without trace.

Is healing one of the steps on love? Frankly, I'm not sure, yet it's such an intrinsic aspect of loving someone and being loved in return, I give it a special place as both a step and an inspired reward. I suppose one has to be hurt before he or she can be healed. Here I'm inclined toward healing as comfort, tranquility, gentleness, peace of mind and heart.

It's not that seniors necessarily were physically injured or abused in a previous relationship, although they may have been; I'm concerned here with the emotional pain which is far longer lasting, and that's where healing is so meaningful.

If you have been successful in taking the steps of love, the reasons for that pain have been relegated to the past where they belong, not forgotten but no longer inflicting agony. You've banished the unpleasant past from the present, and you exist in the present while planning for the future.

How easy it is to say that; how hard it is to deny the earlier reality. That's one reason why sharing fears and doubts with your partner is so important. Out in the open, they are easier to deal with, and dealing with doubt and fear and their causes means you are more relaxed and better able to experience the joy of loving and living.

Healing, I judge, comes to us on two levels. First, it restores our sense of self worth and gives health to our egos. We are someone who can be loved as we are, for ourselves, without mask or pretense. Our sense of ourselves as worthy of being loved is put right. Being loved, we are more complete than we have ever been. We receive respect, someone cares about us, we have value. Not only are we capable of loving and being in love, here, holding our hand, is someone who returns that love and embraces us with his/her heart.

What a wonderful feeling. To know we are wanted is to be touched by a divine hand; to be needed is to be given a spark of holy fire.

Just as I was finishing this book, I was dramatically and movingly reminded of the truth of what I had written above. A small group had enjoyed a dinner at a friend's home. As the last guests were leaving, one of my woman acquaintances said to the hostess, "He was a good man; I still miss him; we had ten wonderful, beautiful years together."

In a moment of open spontaneity she began talking about her late partner. He had died just a year earlier. I don't know the woman very well. I know a long time ago she had been in an abusive marriage and had obtained a divorce; I sense she suffered badly through years of emotional turmoil; for the time I have known her, she has exhibited a marvelously outward upbeat attitude toward life. She works with abused women, dealing with the memory of her own abuse by helping other battered women.

I don't know when she became the partner of her late friend. Years earlier. They never married; they maintained separate homes, but in almost every other way they were a couple, in town and as they traveled throughout the world.

Now, on the anniversary of his death, she felt the need to retell her years of love and happiness. I was sad for her loss and I was envious of her and her partner's precious years of joy.

The emotional scar of her abuse had been healed by love, not forgotten but soothed and calmed. Her sense of failure had been healed by love; she was singularly important in her new man's life. She had achieved a priceless state of well being: she had loved someone and had that love returned. No longer abused, she was honored and respected—and most of all, wanted and needed. And she returned his love in equal measure.

Ten years may not seem like much. In this woman's life the ten years were but fifteen or sixteen percent of her sixty-five. Yet, "I would not trade his love and friendship for anything in this world," she said—and she meant it. She had found happiness with him, and he had helped restore her life. What a blessing their partnership had been. He, too, had needed the healing a loving, caring partner brings to the union of two people, and she had provided that. Their "second chance" had been a true love story.

The other level of healing after restoration is rejuvenation or reinvigoration. The hand, arm, lips, and heart that tenderly touches us and relights the glorious flame of love within gives us new life. As Thomas Moore wrote, "there's nothing half so sweet in life / As love's young dreams."

And there, for seniors, is one of love's healing secrets: we are not made young again; that's impossible; it is our dreams that are perpetually pure and fresh and young.

Healing erases years of toil and hurt. Togetherness gives us that arm-in-arm partner with whom to face life; healing makes us whole and strong again. No words needed. The loving embrace, the loving glance, the presence of love bonds one to the other and helps banish all the thoughts that makes us afraid. We are not alone. We are not frail and weak and helpless; we have been made strong by being loved.

❦　❦　❦

Yet there is a new kind of pain, the pain of loving. Love creates its own pain. It's as simple as "Does he really love me?" or "What would I do if she ever left me?" The pain is stress, an emotional malady that can become physical. Heart, brain and body are subjected to pressures like no others.

Healing comes with the affirmation of love, when your loved one reaffirms love and commitment. We know all about the love-sick youths; we ignore the fact that seniors also can be stricken.

Should a love fail or our loved one be separated from us, time and distance promise some calming balm, but the pain never does go away completely, sometimes not even when we meet another love. There's always that little corner in our hearts where our disappointment lurks.

The acquaintance I've just mentioned unintentionally illustrates the point: a harmful marriage, abuse, followed by divorce; a sense of bitter disappointment and of ego shattering failure; the discovery of a man to love and to be loved by; ten happy, fulfilling, meaningful years; then his death and another separation.

Or perhaps one finds a love that lasts but a brief moment and fails, time being an irrelevant measure of true happiness. Again, the sad separation and loss.

On a balance sheet, an insensitive clod would judge the risk of loss too risky an emotional investment. I can't anticipate your judgment; mine is, even knowing separation is forecast if only by age, that the risk of reaching out for and achieving happiness, even if the love involved fails, is worth every and any effort.

❦ ❦ ❦

Up to now, following the steps of love, the burden of proving love has been on you. If you are fearful, have been disappointed, are stressed by doubt, it's natural. You're doing your part. Keep working on it.

Now you anxiously await the reward for your loving. The reward is not physical but emotional. All the pain of your doubts, worries and stress will be eased by your partner's simple words: "I love you; there is no other. I am in love with you."

That said, a miracle. If you are rewarded with those words, your loved one erases all the pain you have suffered. If you were hurting, the loving words heal. On earth there is nothing more divine than your angel's voice speaking words of love to you alone.

Lovemaking

With eyes and voice, we are love.
Let joys of sight and sound
precede the touch. Rejoice
in the awareness of love.

If you've skipped the preceding chapters to get to this one, you have cheated—yourself and your partner. When you discovered someone and reached out to him/her, the bonds of intimacy were frail and fragile. Taking the steps of love strengthened those bonds. You dealt with each other's fears and doubts, shared your hopes, planned for some kind of future together, reevaluated your love and your goals and encouraged your loved one to do the same, and you made a mutual commitment of love and to a lifetime together.

As you took the steps, your bond grew tighter and more secure. You trusted your partner and received trust in return. You learned to relax and truly began to enjoy the relationship. You became a couple, forged a partnership, pledged to meet and greet life together.

But, if you charged into a sexual relationship too early or entered into a sex only relationship, and providing you want to build such a shallow relationship into something more, go back to the beginning of this book, back at least to reaching out, and create the kind of meaningful, shared, mutual foundation that can bring lasting happiness to both of you. This chapter will wait until you do.

❦ ❦ ❦

Right off I want to announce a radical thought. Having sex *is not* the destination at the end of your love taking steps.

Say that again! Okay. Lovemaking is a step toward a destination.

As important, as special, as meaningful, as unique, as spiritual, as singular, as fulfilling, as desired as it is, making love, the physical act of love however seniors do it, is not the goal or the end purpose of loving.

Touching, holding, fondling, caressing, kissing at whatever level a couple bond physically are demonstrations of something larger and far more important and profound. All of the above are important, very important, but none are the end.

The end or the culmination of a love affair is the love of two people, the meeting, greeting and union of two hearts, neither of which is whole without the other, each of which needs the other to be complete.

The meeting and coupling of two physical bodies is not enough. In love there must be more. Lovemaking follows the creation of an environment of mutuality in which trust and respect and commitment are present, otherwise lovemaking is for one's pleasure at the expense of the other, even if the other is just seeking pleasure also, i.e., casual, recreational sex which has no lasting meaning and makes no commitment.

If love or some imitation of it is not present, how can any sex act reaffirm caring and the sense of union so necessary to a deep and abiding relationship? Sex alone cannot. To use your partner for selfish sexual release is exactly that, using, and, in a very real way, is abuse.

Within the context of all that's been said about building a sound and secure relationship, to end up satisfied
with a moment of casual sex belies every thought of
love.

Love, if there be love, is deeper and more profound.

❦   ❦   ❦

You are a sensual being, have been since before you
were born. In your mother's womb you responded to
certain stimuli: sound, rocking, warmth. As soon as you
were born, you responded to more: touch, being
cleaned and bathed and fed. And not long after, you
responded to still more: sight and colors, smells and
voices.

And the stimuli evoked responses: you touched and
saw, tasted and smelled and heard a whole new world,
and you learned to relate to it through your senses and
to vocalize what you felt, both pleasure and pain.

Once you got accustomed to the new world, you
became aware of your body and explored it—until
someone or a lot of someones told you to stop it and
made a big issue about not touching yourself *down there.*

You weren't doing anything wrong; it was a part of
discovery. It had nothing to do with your sexuality; it
wasn't something "dirty." This is a rug I crawl on, this is a
blanket that keeps me warm, this is my mother's breast
that feeds me, this is my crib, this is my hand, my toe,
my penis or my vagina. This is my world; this is me.
Long before you ever thought about sex, you and your
world were natural, everything accepted for what it

was— natural. You were aware of your genitals and sensed sensual but not yet sexual genital pleasure.

Can you remember your earliest sexual awareness? Probably not. It's more likely that suddenly, or so it seems, you were aware, and ever since then sensuality and sexuality have been unalterably fused. Someone once said that the fusion of sexuality and sensuality is the reward we receive for being human.

❦ ❦ ❦

Lovemaking is a word requiring careful definition. For starters, I choose to spell lovemaking as one word. Some will object, as my computer's spell check does, wanting it to be two separate words; others will want to make a hyphenated word, "love-making." I don't want a hyphen; I don't want two words, either, because love-making on all its levels and in all its potential forms is a singular physical and emotional expression of one's love. Let nothing, not hyphenating or splitting the words, suggest that lovemaking is other than the complete and total physical and emotional union of two persons.

You will take good care of the word(s) in your own way; I want only that you understand what I say: making love is a singular physical as well as an emotional expression of love; how a couple makes love may be as varied as there are couples.

In lovemaking there are no norms, nothing is "normal," not frequency, time of day or night, setting, means and/or techniques. Certain "facts" are reported as "on the average," but everything is misleading and useless. Your sex life is what you and your partner make it. The when, where and how are up to you and him/her. Again, all's fair that is mutual and without force.

So let's start somewhere back down along the steps you have taken. At some point you and your loved one became a couple. You looked into each other's eyes, you touched each other, held hands; your hearts embraced the other's heart; you spoke about the future; you formed a bond and committed yourselves to a union; you hugged and kissed, tentatively at first, then with passion. In the beginning of your relationship the only questions was, "How far should I go?" or "How far should I let myself go?" You were young again; your heart raced; your heart lead your mind, "I love him/her. I want us to be one."

You were a sensual child again: you craved what your eyes saw and your fingers touched, what your ears heard and your nose smelled and your tongue tasted. You wanted to be held, kissed, felt.

You wanted to—but you were afraid to.

Seniors have fears. "If I get too close to you, I'm dependent on you." "If we should be separated, what would I do?" "I'm afraid to risk it." "Tell me you love me;" "touch me; leave me alone;" "love me but don't be in love with me;" "hold me but don't caress me;" "I want to, but I don't dare."

We long for intimacy—and deny it.

❦   ❦   ❦

A while ago a woman told me, "Things are going so well, I know something bad will happen," a form of self-fulfilling prophecy. And so she manufactures excuses for holding her would-be lover at arm's length. I know she is afraid, not only of external bad things but of him, not that he might do her physical harm but that she will become too dependent on him or that he will become the single focus of her life.

So instead of closeness, she brings up things that pain and disturb her and develops little arguments in which her partner can't possibly hope to hold his own, and when she does either of those things, he's not able to change her mood. She's not aware of what she is doing; it's an unconscious protective defense mechanism that works. Focusing on something disturbing and transferring that negativism to him means she does not have to focus on him as a person to love; he can hold her but not touch her; he can love her but must not be in love with her.

She does not accept the very thing that might ease her pain, the presence of someone who loves her and who wants to bear her burdens and help lighten the load she carries. She doesn't dare the closeness.

She hasn't learned to enjoy joy.

Gender has nothing to do with it. I know as many unrealized males as I do females, and in some instances the males have more difficulty because they have been raised culturally to avoid displays of closeness and to keep everything locked inside themselves.

"Men don't cry" is nonsense. Men cry, and men cry out. From the tips of their toes to the tops of their heads they are as much a sensual being as any woman—and like some women, they are afraid to relax and enjoy.

Or enjoyment brings forth guilt. Not that someone is injured but as in, "I don't deserve such happiness" or "I have no right to accept happiness; something bad will happen to destroy it."

Guilt and fear become a mishmash of emotional conflict, sometimes to the point where one partner wishes to dissolve the partnership. "I don't want him/her to love me." If such negative thoughts are present, they must be confronted and attended to forthwith and forthrightly. If the couple cannot deal with the fact and its implications, by the time professional help is considered, it may be too late to rescue the relationship.

And often the failure is because the fear of enjoyment stresses one with guilt. Deciding not to make love, one dismisses love also, a devastating combination.

❦ ❦ ❦

Let's assume a more favorable climate and an agreeable atmosphere.

In the mysterious ways things are categorized, by consensus, mid-life is thought to be that age between forty and sixty-five and old age anything thereafter.

Psychologically, it's an arbitrary division. Physiologically it has validity. Physical changes are too numerous to begin to list. Let's take just two by way of example, two that impact directly on lovemaking. Women will experience vaginal changes, e.g., loss of vaginal tissue around the pelvic bone and less and delayed vaginal lubrication. The main change for men centers on erectile function, the time it takes to achieve an erection and/or the penis's hardness.

For those seniors about to or engaged in lovemaking, numerous factors come into play simultaneously. The first is recognizing the fact of the body's changes. What does that mean?

For the couple which accepts the fact of aging, one emotional (as well as physical) meaning can be an unparalleled opportunity to fully explore and express sexuality in ways perhaps never before experienced. Once aroused by visual stimuli and erotic thoughts, that may not be enough; direct manual and oral stimulation may be necessary and desired.

If you trust your partner and he/she you, experimentation with ways of touch, position, verbal expressions, and fore and after play may open doors to pleasures heretofore unknown.

Remember, there is a legitimate selfishness inherent in lovemaking: self-satisfaction. You want to give your partner his/her maximum pleasure, and you want the maximum pleasure for yourself.

Giving and receiving maximum pleasures are learned over time. "This is what I like." "Do this." "Show me." "What's the most pleasing thing I can do?"

For seniors, the simple, basic act of intercourse may not be enough. Actually, it should not be enough. Lovemaking may be learning to make love all over again in new, mutually satisfying ways. There's joy in that.

And the joy is not just physical; it's emotional, two people finding in the physical expression of their love the depths to which their hearts and minds unite.

It seems unnecessary, but the question arises: is

lovemaking (sex) good for you? The question is not do you enjoy it but is sex healthy for seniors? The quick answer is yes. The medical and psychiatric professions agree. Intimacy, touch and skin-to-skin contact, petting, and holding close are essential to emotional and physical well being.

But a warning. Sex without love can be psychologically devastating, leaving one depressed and, if the temporary lover leaves, rejected. That kind of sex is joyless.

❦ ❦ ❦

A couple of chapters ago I wrote about touching, physically maintaining contact with your partner. I want to return briefly to that theme.

The physiological changes that happen to our bodies means that in lovemaking we need more time for arousal, and that means more time given to sensuous foreplay and to the sensuality and intimacy of the sexual encounter. Hugging, kissing, cuddling, stroking, manual stimulation, oral stimulation are all ways of expressing love. Touch, however done, is a basic human need. It is of vital importance to babies. At that level, touch is often called "sensual massage," connecting, in this instance, mother and child, reaffirming the bond they experienced when the baby was in the mother's womb.

For centuries, sensual massage was a valuable medical treatment. It relaxed and soothed the patient; it established a connection between the patient and the caregiver. Its practice has disappeared from hospitals now, to the patient's loss.

Couples need sensual massage. Here we're not talking about "sexual massage" that focuses on the genitals; here we're talking about touching and soothing the toes, arms, back of the legs, back, the slow kneading of muscles that relaxes your partner.

There is a reward; giving such a massage allows you to "discover" your partner's body and what feels good to him or her.

For both sexes, the entire body is a sexual organ, the entire skin just as much as the so-called erogenous "spots" or "zones." Sensual massage might lead to sexual massage, but that happens only when the couple wants and allows it to happen.

❦ ❦ ❦

Sexual dysfunction is a major senior concern. There are over two hundred prescription medications available for treating sexual dysfunction, to say nothing of hundreds of non-prescription herbs, lotions and mechanical devices.

For the senior male, there is the unique issue of an erection, or for fifty percent or more of senior males, the lack of one, with or without Viagra and herbs. Erectile dysfunction has been studied and researched endlessly.

Female dysfunction, while not ignored, has received far less attention, a classic disservice to women. In 1999, the "Journal of the American Medical Association" reported that of those women reaching age sixty-five, forty-three percent suffered from some form of sexual dysfunction. As women age, that percentage increases.

There are reasons for the "failure" of the penis to become and/or remain erect: age and/or the body's inability to respond because of vascular, cardiac or prostate problems; medications; fear of physical exertion; emotional "beatings" from long ago; etc. I hate to use etceteras, but the list of potential reasons for erectile dysfunction is beyond the scope of this book. One who "suffers" from the condition should seek the help of his physician—if for no other reason than the underlying cause(s) may reveal far greater life threatening conditions.

That aside, an interesting thing with many men: the heart and brain are stimulated, and even though the penis doesn't respond, the brain says it has. Only when a man checks, does he discover he is flaccid.

The lack of an erection is not failure, although many men consider it their failure and thus will avoid making the ultimate physical contact with their partner, watching television endlessly, playing infinite numbers of computer games, finding excuses or distressing ideas to divert both self and partner away from lovemaking.

If an erection is considered proof of a man's vitality and there is no erection, or it doesn't last, the man is defeated; his ego suffers an incalculable blow to his self esteem. He is not a man; he is humiliated. Within a loving relationship, that's a lot of needless pain and suffering.

If a male fails to achieve an erection, the female may also suffer, not once but twice. First, she may believe she is not able to "turn on" her mate and therefore, in some way, she is responsible for his inability to have an erection. Her self-esteem is lowered. Again, needless emotional suffering.

Second, if she is aroused, and the male cannot "perform," her sexual needs may not be satisfied. More needless suffering.

The view that the male's lack of or brief lasting erection precludes sensuality and sexuality is utterly false. Sexual sensuality begins with love, and as the Roman philosopher Ovid, said, "Love must be fostered by soft words." The great nineteenth century Russian writer, Alexander Pushkin, said that Ovid sang "The science of the tender passion." To put it less poetically and more bluntly, sexual activity begins long before you get to the bedroom. First the words and actions expressing love, then the caresses.

And although neither Ovid nor Pushkin mention it, nor for that matter do many counselors, the testosterone effects that struck a young boy and the body's sexual urges that came upon a young woman may, as physical manifestations, diminish with age. Women know that with menopause their body's production of progesterone ceases.

By the time a woman achieves the status of senior, usually most of the physical issues of menopause and perimenopause are moot (setting aside the realistic concerns about osteoporosis). Reproductive availabilities are absent, one of nature's distinction between male and female.

Menopause is an event, although perimenopause may cover a length of time. The male's loss of reproductive abilities may never happen completely; his diminishing ability is not an event but an episode stretched out over dozens, even scores, of years.

Hormonal changes take place in both female and male. It is natural.

One thing that is not natural is regarding menopause (and pregnancy and a woman's monthly cycle) as a disease. The point I want to make here is that nature has determined the hormonal changes in our bodies. It has not determined our beliefs, so many of them myths, about the end of sensuality and sexuality.

An astonishing truth: what began as a physical coming of age for the body becomes an emotional reality (need) that lasts a lifetime. And that's entirely normal too.

An old woman looks at a man and sees in him something that stirs her. Her body reacts. More significantly, so does her mind (and in the poet's language, so does her heart). Her lovemaking days have passed, she says, but her emotional days of response have not. Unless she deliberately excludes such thoughts from her life, she is young again. The flesh may be weak but the spirit is willing, eager even. Age is no factor. So, too, for the aged male. His testosterone levels may have hit rock bottom, or so he thinks, but responding to an attractive female gives the lie to the belief that he is incapable of expressing love.

What a mistake seniors make who believe their lovemaking days are over. It's so only if you choose to believe the falsity.

Whether the male has an erection is not the "macho" concern some make it. A man can arouse a woman and maintain her level of excitement in so many other ways, and if the man and woman are free of inhibitions and fears, she will focus on her own psychological and physiological needs and pleasures and respond to the male— and he to her.

That depends largely on whether they have successfully taken the steps of sharing, committing and relaxing. There are ways for the soft penis to be as exciting and arousing as the hard penis. And both man and woman should be aware: the flaccid penis is still an erogenous zone.

Here, sharing becomes more than an ideal; it becomes a sensual reality. If the male cannot ejaculate, his mate's orgasm becomes *our* orgasm. There is no you or me in lovemaking, only us.

Women, too, have "inabilities." Age affects women every bit as much as it affects men. They may not lubricate; because of such conditions as endometriosis, yeast infections, dyspareunia, interstitial cystitis, vulvodynia, low testosterone levels, etc., intercourse may be so painful as to be physically impossible; surgery may have taken an unavoidable toll. As for men, women should seek professional (gynecologist) advice and possible treatment.

Intercourse is not always necessary; the holding, cuddling, voiced reassurances are what's important. Given the issue(s), the question is, is the man or woman, then, less than sensuous or less desirable? Certainly not. There are a thousand ways to be pleased and a thousand ways to give pleasure.

Many men receive pleasure just seeing their partner,

looking into her eyes, looking at her body. It used to be suggested that women got little pleasure from looking at a man, that they'd rather read about what a man does. I don't know where that idea originated, probably in an earlier, misguided age when women weren't supposed to have erotic thoughts.

Nevertheless, let both of you *read* the love your bodies write, what is written in your eyes, what is translated into feelings by what you do physically to reassure your loved one of your love. Don't hide behind excuses or use your limitations to avoid making love.

Whatever happens at whatever level, both can enjoy their lovemaking and its physical passion. The reward is immense: a sense of oneness, a sense of stability and security and safety, comfort, self acceptance, love. Above all, love. Everything starts with love, and it ends with love. That's the wonder of being a loving couple.

But, but, but…. I've spoken of this before. Suppose physical lovemaking is beyond reach. What if medications and creams don't help either the man or the woman, that there are no orgasms whatever the reason? What then? What if age precludes the physical fulfillment of sexual fantasies?

Yes, what if?

If you have to ask, you haven't been paying attention. I knew a couple who had been married for seventy-two years. I've heard of longer marriages but personally know of no couple married longer.

I attended their anniversary party. The woman was ninety-eight; her husband was ninety-nine. In the language of their youth, they were dressed "to the nines." They showed their age; they had spent the first eighty years of their lives on the farm. Now, after years of backbreaking work, they seemed frail. Like children, they had to be put to bed and gotten up and helped with their dressing. Yet, when I looked into their eyes, they were young again. I watched them with each other. Their faces spoke of love undimmed by the years. The man did not see a ninety-eight year old woman; he saw his beautiful bride of seventy-two years ago. The woman did not see a man just shy of a hundred; she saw her handsome lover. It was there, the way they looked at each other, the touches that were a lover's caress. Their body language was of youth and of love's beginnings. After all those years, they were still in love.

When was the last time they made love? In their own way they were still making love: the words, the touches, the embraces, the lively eyes conveyed love from one to the other. I have never forgotten them or the lesson they taught: love is expressed in a hundred different ways and love is responded to by just as many.

The days for intercourse have passed? It happens. Whether it is *the* major issue in a loving relationship depends on whether the couple can find meaningful and fulfilling ways to express the physical aspect of their love and whether their love is buttressed securely by trust and faith in one another, because love is more and deeper than the sex act. Love is the emotional flame that ignites two hearts; love is the afterglow that binds two lovers together.

In a long poem he called *The Extasie* John Donne wrote, "Loves mysteries in soules doe grow, / But yet the body is his booke." You'd have to go to the complete poem, but in part, Donne was telling us that carnal, sensual, physical love is inseparable from spiritual love, spirit as in the soul, if you will.

A greater point, Donne knew, is that "the body is his [love's] booke." The mind is of the body, and there we store all that is said and given to us, and thus our whole body is a book whereof our partner in love can read what we write. It's called the body language of love, and if you have taken the steps of love carefully, that book is among the most sacred in the world, however we turn the pages.

❧   ❧   ❧

Making love is a private matter, okay and natural within the context of a loving partnership, filled with light and beauty. When I began this chapter, I wanted lovemaking, at whatever level and however practiced, to be a firework step of your and your loved one's discovery of each other. From the first glance and awareness of someone to the passionate embrace and fulfillment of your union, I wanted only wonder and joy. I wanted that to be your reality. Good things do happen, and if you are blessed with the love of a good and faithful partner, you will know the joy. Express love every day. With your eyes and voice, with your limbs, with every fiber of your body, express your love. Let your senses receive the scents of love issued to you alone. Let your arms and your heart embrace your love. Be enwrapped in your partner's love. Hold each other. Make love, and in the making, take the last step and sing your glorious love song.

Singing

Love itself is a song,
earthy and heavenly
all at once, from one heart
to another. Live long
with me, it sings, and be
what I dreamed from the first:
friend, lover, comforter.
The same is pledged by me.
Let us sing for us two,
not for our yesterdays
but for tomorrow when
love can fulfill anew.

You hold your lover in your arms; you kiss his or her cheeks, hands, chest. Your hands touch and caress the whole body. You say loving words.

You are held, hugged, kissed, hear loving words.

Your world is being put right.

You and your partner have reaffirmed your oneness. You make love in ways that fill both with joy. And in the words of Shakespeare, "the voice of all the gods / make heaven drowsy with the harmony."

Love is your song, the duet you sing with your partner. It is heavenly music sung from one heart to the other. Harmony. Others sing their songs, but none sing your song, nor do they sing to your beloved or to you, nor you to them. What you sing is for two, for you, from you, to your loved one. What he/she sings is for you, to you alone.

You sing loudly and lustily of love and for all your tomorrows. You sing of hope for what tomorrow will bring. You sing of dreams fulfilled and of newness in your new dreaming. You sing because of him, because of her. You sing because he/she loves you. You sing for pains eased. You sing for friendship and partnership; you sing for shared lives. You sing because you are one, and in that oneness no greater song can be imagined.

You sing for joy.

You sing for the pure joy of singing

You sing because of him/her.

You sing to him/her alone. From all this world, you have found the one who makes your heart sing.

You hear love songs.

You hear love songs sung for you, joyous songs of faith and hope. You are my beloved, the songs say; you are mine alone.

Too romantic? Unreal? No one can hope to achieve such happiness? Get real. Look at the lines on your face, look at the age spots on your hands, think about your creaky knees, the thinning (if not absent) hair, the pills on the bathroom shelf, the glasses you have to wear.

Glasses. Not rose colored. Real, thick, the only thing that keeps the world from being one gigantic blur.

Some kind of love might be okay for the elderly, but romance?

Romance is for...the romantic heart. An individual heart, your heart, my heart, may be old mechanically.

That's a biological factor. But spiritually? The heart knows no season nor does it age. See a painting that moves you, hear music that stirs you, read a story that thrills you, smell a flower that recalls a sublime moment, touch an object whose shape and form sends goose bumps all over your body—do you say to the painting or the music or the object, I'm too old to appreciate you? Of course not.

Chances are what moves and thrills you is more valuable, more real because you know just how precious such things are. Age makes us more aware of the gifts of life, not less.

To be given someone's love is to be offered life's greatest gift; bestowing love is the greatest gift we can render. We have been given and give in return the whole person.

So, why settle for the mundane when you can reach for the stars and the moon? And if you can reach toward the heavens, why not reach for the sun, that someone who gives light and warmth to your life? In her poem "The Beautiful Pain of Too Much," Susan Firer begins with these touching lines: "The body memorizes / the place of rapture...."

Think about that for a moment. The older one gets the more deeply one feels. Time has something to do with that; you don't want to waste what's left while you're still young enough to make the most of it. There is no substitute for that one who loves you.

Or is there?

My whole emphasis here has been on finding and

holding someone "more precious than rubies." Continuing that theme, you're never too old; it's never too late. Look around you. See the seniors who have found love and bask in its glow. Life is most complete when there is someone to love and someone to love you in return. Your soul mate, your true friend: find that someone and you will sing forever.

Once, forever was forever, or at least it was a long time. Now, for seniors, the end of forever is just over the horizon, not yet in sight but within reach.

That should make us realize just how carefully we must nurture our love relationship. Time for repairing slights and oversights and hurt feelings, no matter how unintended they are, just isn't there. "I'll patch things up tomorrow" may be too late. Seniors have a finite number of tomorrows. Senior love is not quite as simple as "Eat, drink and be merry, for tomorrow we die." That hedonistic bit of doggerel has no regard for anything except gluttonous pleasure.

Believe me, there is nothing wrong with pleasure (and I hope to have much of it), but pleasure is not happiness. Many people seek numerous pleasures, thinking they'll find happiness, and when they're still not happy, they seek more pleasure, and all the while happiness eludes them and becomes more unattainable.

That's because seeking pleasure can become an enterprise of pure selfishness, and the selfish person is incapable of giving love. Go back a few pages to those people who would rather be wealthy than be in love: the self cannot make room for anything or anyone else.

Eat, drink and be merry? Of course, but not as the central focus of one's life, and certainly not because one simply does not care about tomorrow.

Now, if it seems we've come a long way from singing and forever, we haven't. For seniors there is not a great amount of time left in which to find one's happiness. As pointedly as I can, I suggest that true happiness is not to be found in the material world (money and such) but in the spiritual, by which I specifically mean the environment of love and affection, caring and sharing, the "beautiful years" my female acquaintance referred to earlier in the chapter headed "Healing."

Further, I suggest that a loving couple are the richest people in the world. I hope you find that to be true.

❦ ❦ ❦

More years ago than I sometimes care to remember, I had a friend who was a bass player with the Chautauqua Symphony and an occasional substitute with the Buffalo Symphony. When I could, I would go to the weekly final rehearsals at Chautauqua. On one occasion, a pianist (I'm embarrassed to admit I have forgotten his name) addressed the orchestra. In essence what he said was this: "I like the final rehearsal best of all. Tomorrow we'll be dressed formally and play for the enjoyment of an audience, hoping we inspire or comfort or thrill people who will judge our performance. Now we play only for ourselves and for each other. We're not trying to impress anyone; we're playing for the pure joy of making our instruments sing. If we're lucky, that joy of making music will carry over to tomorrow and make other people happy. But now I play just for you, as you play just for me."

There was more, but that's what I remember, and I've long thought of it as a metaphorical statement. Partners and lovers have their public face and voice, but their most precious music is sung in private and for each other. When what they sing is true, when what they sing is in harmony, it is sublime.

❦ ❦ ❦

Not everyone, not every potential couple, will complete the steps of love. Many will be brought up short by their honest reality check and will not achieve lasting commitment, all their heady plans put on hold.

Some will remain friends, and one of them will wrestle with the frustrations that being in love presents. Does that mean the steps of love were invalid and failed? I don't think so, although obviously they were not completed. If that is your situation, you had the stars for a while; you wanted the moon. You don't love him/her less; you have to prove that differently than you imagined and from afar, and yet... there is friendship and a measure of closeness and perhaps one day....

Love gives strength.

The steps of love are not invalidated by an individual's failure. You and I are sensual beings; we love, perhaps not always wisely, perhaps hopelessly, but we are moved by love. To have someone to love is good; to have someone love us back is grand. There is still time. Maybe....

Most likely not.

Love is not an illusion, a false or mistaken reality. Love is a dream, "a wish your heart makes," to use a little Cricket's song. Perhaps you wished and awoke too soon from your dream. I so hoped all your wonderful dreams would come true, and if you had color filled illusions, I wished they had become your exquisite reality.

You dared to love; dared to be loved; dared to open your heart, and if there were risks, you dared them also. Being in love and being loved are emotions too precious to waste. You trusted yourself; you listened to your heart, your inner voice. You said the words, "I love you." You proved it every day. It was not enough.

Have faith; love does win—sometimes.

If you and your partner are joined in song, you have been blessed by life's greatest gift. You may not be materially rich, you may not be in prime health, you may not be the king or queen of the universe, you may be one of the world's average everyday human entities without fame, but being loved, you are rich beyond price, strong beyond compare, secure beyond defeat. You are a special someone because you have been made complete. You are loved and you have someone to love; life's supreme achievement is yours. Give thanks for that. Touch your loved one tenderly and tell him/her again and again, "I am in love with you, my dearest one." The song you hear returned will be one of faith and hope and courage—and of love. You will be rich beyond your wildest dreams.

A Delicate Balance

Actually, I can't ever remember anyone who sought my help asking to see my degrees or even asking what I knew about parenting or marital conflict or financial difficulties or career changes or death or fear or ego or failure or abuse or about any of the myriad difficult life areas in which one needed help.

Specifically, since this book is about seniors and love, I don't ever remember anyone asking what I know about being older and being in love.

If someone had asked what I knew about love, for instance, I'm not sure what I would have told them, if in fact I could have told them anything they didn't already know. Anyway, that's not the way most counseling works. When someone sought my help, he or she was not testing my knowledge, but was, in a way, challenging my ability to help them discover how to deal with their concern(s) and help them find ways to cope with their unique and intensely personal situation. We don't "fix" people; counselors strive to help people understand themselves, how they got into their predicament in the first place and how they might deal with and solve, or at least handle, it.

As regards love, I never did, but I might have read these lines: "Required in every good lover," wrote Miguel de Cervantes in his epic *Don Quixote*, "the whole alphabet... Agreeable, Bountiful, Constant, Dutiful, Easy, Faithful, Gallant, Honourable, Ingenious,

Kind, Loyal, Mild, Noble, Officious, Prudent, Quiet, Rich, Secret, True, Valiant, Wise... Young and Zealous."

Think about what the words meant when Cervantes wrote them in the sixteenth century, remembering that he wrote in Spanish and that his 1500's Spanish was translated into seventeenth century English (the King's kind). Words such as "officious" and "rich" had different meanings then, gentle guidance and spiritual depth, respectively. "Secret" meant not gossiping or telling tales out of school. In other words, love and love activity was a private matter between two people. "Easy" meant flexible, able to maintain an even disposition no matter the stresses of life. Other than understanding the then meaning of the words, the list summarizes what one must offer when one offers his/her love. And love was what Don Quixote was about.

If I could, I would make Cervantes' list a premarital test. One either passes or fails, receives an A or an F. To fail even one quality required in every lover throws all qualities into doubt. If one is not Agreeable, how then can one be Kind? If one is not Faithful, how can one be True? If not Noble, how can one be Honourable?

And now look at the list of words again. It is the qualities of the best of humans in every facet of daily living.

The letters "u," "j" and "x" are missing from the English rendition. Don Quixote, The Knight of the Woeful Figure (or Rueful Countenance) certainly exhibits "unselfishness" and was "just," that word meaning fair, even handed treatment of others (especially one's love) and treating others, including one's love, as equal.

"X" we might consider as an unknown quality, the unalphabetized intangible "something" that exists but cannot be named. "Why do you love me?" "I don't know," meaning what is felt cannot be verbalized easily. Or, "Prove your love." "Well, I'm agreeable ... kind ... true ... and...." "X" is that something other.

There is nothing new in this.

I have among my books the *Cyclopaedia of American Literature* first published in 1855 by Charles Scribner, with an appendix published in 1866, two thousand nine by twelve pages of six point type. Tough going but interesting reading.

For *Seniors in Love* I studied the earliest American writers, hoping for an early love poem or even a reference to romantic love in the colonies and before the colonies of Virginia and Massachusetts. Alas, I found none, only references to those punished for public displays of affection and/or metaphors and/or similes alluding to love, usually by invoking Greek or Roman gods or goddesses known for affairs of the heart. I'm quick to point out that the likes of Eros and Cupid and Venus were not mentioned. Whatever else, early Americans did not talk about love and sex in their literature.

Not so the early American theater, although for reasons beyond my comprehension, plays are not usually considered literature. "The Prince of Parthia" by Thomas Godfrey, written sometime in the 1750's, is credited with being the first play written by an American to be performed in America. The play deals with adultery and rape as well as love on a higher level. Rape is described with these words: "And took those means to force me to his arms."

The King's excuse for his adultery is familiar: "Why should I blush, if heav'n / Has made me as I am, and gave me passions? / Blest only in variety, then blame / The Gods who form'd my nature thus, not me."

To which the cheated-on Queen replied, "… But, yet, revenge, our Sex's joy is mine…." I've heard those words before.

"Banned in Boston" became a joke, if a serious one. Before the American Revolution, theaters themselves were banned in many of the colonies. Many a European play was produced and many of them were acted out in barns and warehouses before secretly selected audiences. (The second play written by an American for American audiences wasn't written until 1787, "The Contrast" by Royall Tyler.)

Our Puritan forefathers (no one knows the views of our foremothers) had some very dark and unnatural views of proper conduct. For instance, although John Calvin, a prime mover of the Puritan movement, celebrated Christmas in Geneva, his English disciples erased that day from their calendar. In the Massachusetts Records of May 11, 1659 appears the following statue:

For preventing disorders arising in several places within this jurisdiction, by reason of some still

observing such festivals such as were
superstitiously kept in other countries to the great
dishonor of God and often to others, it is
therefore ordered by the Court and the authority
thereof, that whosoever shall be found observing
any such day as Christmas or the like, either by
forbearing of labour, feasting, or any other way,
upon such accounts as aforesaid, every such
person so offending shall pay for every such
offence five shillings as a fine to the county.

That's a piece of civil/religious history. The depth of the
Puritan effort to avoid "the facts of life," "the birds and
bees" stuff, is illustrated by the Puritan prohibition of
the solemnization of marriage by the clergy.

(Saint) Paul in his first letter to the Corinthians had
said, "If they cannot contain (themselves), let them
marry: for it is better to marry than to burn (in hell)."
(I Cor. 7:9) (Of course, Paul said some other things: "Let
your women keep silence," "the head of the woman is
the man," and "woman is the glory of the man," words
hardly conducive to equality and partnership.)

In this new land (of religious freedom?), marriage
was considered too worldly a thing for the clerical stamp
of approval. Peter Hobart, minister in Hingham,
Massachusetts, part of the Plymouth Colony, from 1635
to 1678-9, where I used to live (No, not during his
ministry! But more on my age later) was severely taken
to task for solemnizing a marriage in Boston, way up in
the Bay Colony.

Of Hobart's transgression, John Winthrop, then Governor of the Plymouth Colony, wrote, "We were not willing to bring in the English custom of ministers preforming (*sic*) it (marriage)."

How divorced from reality could the clergy get? Early ministers married, some several times, and most fathered children, often lots of them. One wonders about the mind set of the Puritans when it came to sex. Did they claim virgin births and immaculate conceptions? There's no record of that in our country's history when the church and the state were one and the same, only the record of marriages and births. I guess, as Paul said, marriage was better than burning.

Such was the Puritan influence. Even now, seeking early expressions of love, one feels like a Peeping Tom voyeur. Not in their literature but in their history, one finds Pilgrim and Puritan behavior to be not quite so asexual. In the fall of 1621, Myles Standish led an exploration up from Plymouth to Boston Harbor. There on a beach the men encountered a large group of Indian women, most of them young and all wearing clothing made from beaver pelts. Somehow, the Pilgrims managed to get the women to undress. It's not reported what next took place, only that after enjoying the sight, the Pilgrims took all of the clothing, they being in the fur trading business.

And, of course, there was the settlement at Mount Wallaston, "Ma-re Mount" (later known as Merry Mount), where Thomas Morton led men (and women, we suppose) in drunken dances around a May pole.

The Pilgrims and later the Puritans never drank water. Babies, children and adults drank beer, first what had been brought to America on the Mayflower, later with what they made. Beyond their own houses and small barns, what next was built was not a house of worship but a tavern. Ain't we got fun!

But none of this local stuff worked its way into early literature, and in a sense it's a shame, because in total we have been prevented from knowing the early Americans, warts and all. We see them now dressed in black and white (that was Sunday dress only), severe, humorless, dour, unloving, and unnatural, when the truth is they were both religious seekers and businessmen (women being underrated and member of neither church nor parish), and behaved as such, human beings thinking and doing human things.

Anyway, Americans who wanted to write about romantic love went to Wales or France, Italy or Spain. There the romantic literature nourished primarily by the Greeks flourished.

It took two hundred years for American literature to catch up, when Walt Whitman celebrated America and in so doing celebrated love, heterosexual and homosexual. What the Englishman Havelock Ellis did for sex, Whitman did for love. He took the pioneering, muscled, stoic hero and the daring, long suffering heroine and created heroes and heroines tender in their passion and faithful to their vows. Wives became as important as husbands; mothers became as important as fathers; daughters became as important as sons. By the long strokes of his pen, Whitman gave the sexes equality and from a man and a woman created a partnership, first family, then community, then nation.

Of course there were novels and poems available in early America which dealt with love (and some descriptive sex), but they were borrowed and translated from Europe, conception, content and style, the thought being, apparently, that the continent (the one across the sea) was doing it all.

You'll protest re. Whitman. What about Nathaniel Hawthorne's *The Scarlet Letter*? Well, there's no love in that story, only adulterous sex between a married woman and, we find out later, a clergyman, and a child, the child proof of the sex, the woman's husband long away. That brief encounter doesn't pass as love, nor did Hawthorne intend it to. The hero/heroine of the story is not Hester or the pilloried minister; it is the letter A itself. The demand of colonial Boston for punishment, the stern retribution for sin, is the closest Hawthorne comes to passion: the love of persecuting the sinful.

Students of American literature will ask about James Fenimore Cooper, one of the so-called romantics. "Romantic" had a different meaning back in the early 1800's. Romantic meant manly, adventurous, fighting the Indian kind of stuff. What about Richard Henry Wilde, then? He had some romance poems. Indeed he did, translations. Even John Smith's story of Pocahontas, romanticized by later generations, doesn't qualify. To Smith it was just an incident of fear for his life. Who knows what the Indian maiden felt. Beyond cradling his

about-to-be-bashed-in head in her arms, there was
nothing more. Smith was up and away. It isn't that early
Americans didn't love and lust and seek the pleasures of
the flesh, it's that none of the early writers in America
wrote about such things. We know it isn't so, but colonial America was asexual and love was absent, if we
depend on its literature for knowledge.

Yet what we know of our earliest human history does
come from picture writings, hieroglyphic and cunei-
form, long before any recognizable (to us) alphabet
appeared. And always, as far.back as we can reach, there
was poetry, singing and songs about life: the Sanskrit
"Look to this day...." and the Egyptian "Hymn to the
Sun." There were Buddhist chants and Taoist songs and
Mayan hymns and Hebrew kinahs. Some of the songs
were of joy; some were lamentations or dirges.

And some were about love, manly/womanly love. As
a familiar song reminds us, "the fundamental things
apply / as time goes by."

> …your embraces
> alone give life to my heart;
> may Amun give me what I have found
> for all eternity.

The thought is familiar, although those lines are from
Song no. 2, "Love Songs of the New Kingdom" of
Egypt, composed more than six thousand years ago by
someone who felt what you have felt and may be feeling
now. As I've said before, it's not love that is unique, it's
your love that is unique. You and he; you and she. And
sing about that humanity has.

In the introduction to a collection of the best songs of the 20's and 30's, Richard Rogers wrote, "Setting words to music... it may be that we can sing what we often cannot say, whether it be from shyness, fear, lack of the right words or the passion or dramatic gifts to express them.

"Music... is the 'food of love.'

"Music evokes memories of the past, speaks in tones of the present, and inspires the future."

I choose songs from that era for two reasons. First, because most of us were born in the 20s and 30s, and many of the songs from those years have enjoyed and will continue to enjoy long life. Most of the songs of the twenties were written before I was born, when life must have been gay and innocent and carefree. One of those songs advises, "Don't wash the dishes / just throw them out / Ain't We Got Fun!" Women were "Wild About Harry"; men pined for their sweetie in "Carolina in the Morning." Lovers were also "My Buddy." There was "Barney Google" and "Hard Hearted Hannah" and Sally. What became of her? There was "The Man I Love" and love that failed. "Am I Blue?" Please, "Cuando Vuelvas A Mi" (Spanish for "Lover, Come Back to Me!").

Second, singing is a form of remembering, reflecting, praising, connecting through our senses to sometimes forgotten or ignored feelings within ourselves. We don't sing to perform; we sing to express love, wonder, joy, fear, doubt, surprise, and hope. We may be atonal, but who cares. We are singing the rhythms of our lives and when we do, we become the harmonies. The intellect gives way to the heart, sometimes a joyous heart, sometimes a broken heart

Singing is primal and universal. Love is universal and timeless, as the Egyptian song proves. And so is failed love.

1929 and 30 marked a subtle change in popular love songs. Perhaps because of the Depression there were more songs about failed or unreturned love. "Body and Soul," "But Not for Me," "Dancing With Tears in My Eyes," "Please Don't Talk About Me When I'm Gone," "Something to Remember You By," and "I Guess I'll Have to Change My Plan." I wonder sometimes if seniors who reach out for a second chance at love take it harder when that love fails simply because they were brought up on a diet of blue and torch songs.

At the time it was almost as though there was a sudden meteoric rush of reality. Of course, "it" still happened. "Zing! Went the Strings of My Heart," and one could sing "I Got Rhythm" because you're "Too Marvelous for Words."

That was then; this is now. On the long path of your life, you've not been here before with this person. Everything is new and fresh, pure and full of promise. And still we sing.

It was early in my ministerial career. An older woman member of my new congregation was going to remarry. She and her future husband wanted me to lead them through the exchange of their vows. I was pleased to be asked.

"There are a couple of problems," the woman told me. "I want to be married in the church. You know, walk down the aisle, the whole bit."

"That's no problem," I said. "What's your concern?"

"My ex-husband."

She and her husband had divorced years before I knew them. Both had remained church members and on the surface, at least, seemed to be casual friends. I knew her only as a member of the congregation. Her ex-husband I knew both as a member of the congregation and as a fellow participant in some community projects. But I hadn't been in that church very long and I didn't know either very well and knew nothing of their past history.

"He'll resent a big church wedding."

I wondered about that. "I'll talk with him," I offered.

"And I want to wear a white gown."

I said okay spontaneously. Seldom was I invited to opinionate on wedding costumes.

"You don't object? White is a symbol of virginity. My ex will object."

"It's your wedding," I told the couple. "People who attend are your invited guests, and they accept the invitation to express their happiness for you. They want to share in your joy." And I spoke other noncommittal words. I left unspoken my lack of concern for the color of the bride's gown.

I learned more when I spoke with the ex-husband: an impulsive wartime marriage, four years of separation, reluctant fidelity on his part, no question about hers, a marriage that failed, no one's fault, an agreeable separation, and, finally, an amicable divorce.

"I wish her well; she wanted a church wedding; white is appropriate; it's her new beginning."

Then he added almost as an afterthought, "I'm not jealous; I'm a homosexual." He followed up quickly with "I'll even give her away."

I did not know about his sexuality. Later, he told me that was the first time he ever had uttered those words. But that's another story.

The wedding went as planned, beautiful white wedding gown and all. The bride looked her sixtyish, but her age lines and especially her eyes radiated in the glow of love. Her ex-husband was an invited guest, a friend who for reasons beyond her control (and perhaps beyond her knowledge or understanding) never could have been her lover.

There were a few who commented on the color of her gown, one a thrice married woman who announced that if she married again, she'd wear black. (She did marry again and wore a robin's egg blue dress. I remember the color because I remembered her uncouth remark.)

I have been privileged to participate in numerous elderly couple's weddings. I'm no color expert, and quite frankly, I don't care if the bridal dress is beige, pink, blue, or white. And I don't search for subtle meanings in the dress or gown's color.

The fact is, I like white wedding attire, virginity or the lack of it not withstanding. (If that was the test, by today's standards few brides could wear white.) Let the viewer interpret the color(s) as he or she will. For my part, white is symbolic of the purist intents, the greatest hopes, the enduring promises, the everlasting vows. I would dress the groom in white, or plenty of it anyway, for the same reason.

The reception was a church and community family affair with a small combo that played music from the twenties and thirties, love songs that seemed to express the couple's deepest and truest emotions. At one point the groom told me, "I can't sing. I could kill a choir within minutes, but to me these are sacred songs."

As I write this, I am seventy-five years old. I've sung the songs, both of love and of remorse, and from years ago I agree: they may not be sacred music as we understand the word sacred, but they are spiritual in the sense that song writers have captured our innermost love thoughts, singing for us what we often are unable to say for ourselves.

Singing, and dancing, are the joyous expressions of life. You may sing off key and not in the purest of musical rhythm, but singing to, for and with your loved one is a glorious celebration of who and what you have found.

❧　❧　❧

According to some people, my age explains a lot. They tell me I am out of touch with reality. Specifically regarding sex. I've had young people and middle aged people, even elderly people, propound profusely on sexual activity as creative recreation. Let me present two extreme examples that sometimes mark society's present mood.

I understand the physical need to release pent up physical and emotional tensions. I'm not sure I understand "doing it" with a stranger, although I understand the desired total lack of commitment in such an encounter. To some my disapproval proves just how out of touch I am.

I understand something of the pressures, frustrations and the need for peer protection and approval that leads to same sex group sex, although understanding does not mean approval. And I confess that I do not understand nor do I condone the need for mixed group sex and the exchanging of multiple partners, not one of whom would anyone take home to meet mother. "It's okay," one woman said, "because I only do it when my husband takes part." I am out of touch.

In the counseling situation, one guards against making or appearing to make judgments. Sometimes that's difficult, especially if at issue is unethical, antisocial or destructive behavior. But I never give approval for such activity. That would be reinforcing the already destructive behavior.

I raise the issue of sex again because there is a generational gap plaguing seniors. Our values are at odds with ... our fantasies.

Many seniors are delicately balancing their values and their illusions. We are what we are, but some seniors think that somehow they've missed out or that life has cheated them or that they were born either a generation too late or three or four generations too early.

"Vogue," "Vanity Fair" and a hundred other magazines, and TV, portray the good life as beautifully proportioned young men and women, rich, sexually carefree, charming, in demand. The good life is for those under forty, at least ten pounds under their desired weight, always able to get the prime parking place because being beautiful or handsome in the right clothes and driving the right car and being available for fun and games always wins out.

Not only do seniors lose out by comparison with such images, they are frustrated because the dashing young men and gorgeous women majority pass them by. Seniors are over the hill.

Or so they think.

It's true: paint and primping isn't going to make us one of the beautiful people. Cosmetic surgery might help for a while. If we aren't rich by now, for most of us it's unlikely that we will become so. The race is to the swift, and our fleetness of foot was a half century ago. Sexually? Well, let's just say the days of the rabbit have passed.

Two things, and you know what they are. You just need to be reminded of them and to put them into perspective.

The first is your values, the ethical principles that have guided you (yes, sometimes by violating them) all these years. Go back to Don Quixote. What was alphabetized about love applies to all of life. And if your values are solid and sound, there is no room for envy.

Above all things, maintain your integrity. Only you can compromise your values. There may be great pressure to do so, but in the end it's you who gives truth to what you believe or you who turn your beliefs into lies. Not even a great love should force you to belie those things in which you believe; a worthy lover will not ask that you do.

Second, we are what we are. Face it, the years will not roll away. But know this, too. There is more to every individual than a good body. All bodies age. What doesn't age is intelligence and character, integrity and love. No, you can't see that on the outside, and sometimes inner beauty isn't immediately apparent, but whether you're looking at someone or presenting yourself, what's inside a person will last, solid, secure and, best of all, faithful.

I won't name names, but you can think of stunning movie starlets who in later years look like a truck accident. Conversely, you know nerdish-looking men who turned into handsome older men. Genes? Yes. Living habits? Yes. But mostly it's the inner self showing through the outer self. Whether for good or bad. Don't be fooled by appearance, or try to fool others. In time the truth will out, by which I mean the true person will emerge.

❦ ❦ ❦

Love makes us do some strange things and sometimes leads us down mysterious pathways. We're protected only if we remind ourselves who and what we are. If you say "I love you," you're offering your values and your

integrity to another, and if he/she says "I love you, too,"
you're being offered that person's values and integrity.
Yes, for some love is a charade, a parlor (or bedroom)
game. You don't have to play, although for a time you
may not know it's a game. You cannot control the other
person, just hope, really, that the voicing of love is a fact,
not a weapon of abuse. But you can control your role in
whatever is happening. You start by being honest with
him/her and with yourself; all else goes on from there.

I don't want to get into the realm of personality types
—except this once and because it's pertinent.

Oversimplified, and I stress that, in a love relationship
often there is giving and taking, or to use the crude
analogy of the marketplace, there is buying and
selling... when ideally there should be only barter, the
exchange of equal goods, i.e., "I give you my love and
you give me your love in return;" "I give what I am for
what you are;" "I offer what I have for what you have;"
and "I hand you my hopes and dreams in exchange for
your hopes and dreams," that kind of give and take.

If the bartering works, your hopes and dreams now
include the hopes and dreams of your loved one. Whatever he or she is becomes part of what you are. And thus
the love you give is expanded to an infinite degree
because you receive his/her love in return.

Ideally, I say, and then point out a bump in the road.
Love is not a bunch of grapes or an automobile or an
article of clothing to be sold and bought.

Take, for example and by way of a simple illustration,
the giving/receiving of small gifts.

It's natural, if you come across something your partner might like, to buy it and give it to him or her. It's a token, a thoughtful gift. You derived pleasure when you picked it out and received pleasure when you gave it, and the thanks you got in return made you feel good.

So you continue with the gifts. As the giver, you benefit from the joy of being able to give.

But after a while of giving, there is no reciprocation, no token of exchange, no meaningful acknowledgement of the gifts. You have, through no fault of your intentions, been turned from a giver into a buyer. Your gifts are payment for love.

And the receiver, unconsciously perhaps, has become not just a receiver but a seller. In the extreme, the receiver/seller gives back only to receive friendship or respect or status, or love, and in the end receives none of those things, as in "I gave the teacher an apple and he gave me a D." Selling/receiving has been reduced to attempted bribery.

In the exchange of gifts, the gifts themselves are meaningless. It's the giving that's significant, whether the gift is an article of value or a bunch of wildflowers picked from the side of the road. It is the thought that counts. Too many receivers dismiss the thought or are ignorant of the meaningfulness of the proffered tokens of love.

Basically, nonreciprocating receivers are selfish; they proclaim their generosity, but their generosity is for a reward of some kind, as I've mentioned. I'm always disagreeably surprised when a receiver type personality refuses to consider the consequences of taking only.

Denial is a kind of death wish, the relationship lasting only as long as the gifts keep coming.

No long lasting or healthy relationship can endure if created by one giver and one receiver, one buyer and one seller.

And this is not confined to the love relationship; it impacts friendship, too. It is part of what Cervantes meant by "bountiful." Let me stress that the value of the gifts is irrelevant. It's the exchange and the thought behind the exchange that is meaningful.

❦ ❦ ❦

I want to take from Cervantes another line: "Those two fatal words, Mine and Thine."

I've stressed this before: the truth of love is that there is no mine and thine, no you and me. There is only ours and we, the ultimate commitment of one to the other, for richer, for poor, in sickness or in health....

Life is not fair. Sometimes good things happen to very bad people, and, as we undoubtedly know, bad things happen to some very good people. Let's assume we're all very good people. Tragic things do happen to us or to the one we love. If we do the right things, all should be right with us, or if we behave properly, we can protect our loved ones from harm. Happiness and happy endings should result from our right thoughts, behaviors and actions.

Sometimes our best intentions are not enough; bad things happen. When one loves, the bad things are not your problem or his/her problem, they are our problem. It's easy to face the good times together; it's a true test of love to face the bad times together.

"We" and "our" are, as I have said, love words. Unlike no other words, they link two people together. They are the ultimate words that strengthen the partnership, that each time spoken recreate the sought for bonding.

Robert Moore's male/female archetype models (those original figures or persons after whom we pattern our lives) lists "King/Queen," "Warrior," Magician," "Lover," a strange list when you think about it. Ruler, fighter, trickster, lover? Where's equal partner, communicator, teacher, sharer, explorer? For younger people, where's father, mother, guide, exemplar?

Lover? Okay, give that model the best connotation, but you want your lover to first be in love with you and you with him/her. Real love is a spiritual thought, or should be, before it's a physical happening. The best lover seeks more than sexual gratification, neither yours nor mine. Ours. Ours based on love.

If some of this sounds like preaching, I apologize. It is, of course, in a way, because the best preaching makes us reach into ourselves and helps us rediscover the core values of our lives. The best preaching helps us remember our true selves, and if our remembering is successful, we build on the sound principles garnered from a lifetime of living.

There may be an Islamic, Jewish, Christian, Buddhist, Taoist, etc., etc. bias to our thoughts. We may be theist, agnostic, humanist, or atheist, but within the human heart, expressed by the human spirit, there are universals, values that translate into the best of human behavior, and that best is nowhere more eloquently and sublimely expressed than in the one-to-one exchange of love words.

❦ ❦ ❦

Seniors exist on a delicate balance scale, age on one side, health on the other, or dreams weighed against reality, or risk vs. safety, or faith challenged by doubt.

In ancient Egyptian mythology, when one died, his or her heart was weighed against a feather. If the heart was pure, if the heart had been kind and faithful, loyal and noble, if the heart was filled with love, it balanced the feather. One was in harmony forever with the gods.

The fundamental things do apply.

There are those who close the door against love. One wonders if closing the door is because of fear of what's outside or because of fear of what's inside.

In my counseling I've seen both fears. Either one means—for entirely different reasons—that the light of love is shut out and denied with intensity.

Dealing with either is not easy; both can be devastating. Which is worse, distrust of others or distrust of one's self? I can't answer that; it's a case by case issue; in their extremes, both are personality disorders. If the thought of love ever occurred to such a person, it would be denied; certainly such persons would not be reading a book such as this.

Fortunately, most of us don't suffer such dramatic mental/emotional conditions. We are, however, up on that delicate scale, balancing thoughts about loving against the actual risk of loving.

Perhaps it is a case of getting into harmony with our valued principles, our belief in ourselves as persons of worth and our belief that the vast majority of people are honest, kind, noble, and loving. Earlier in this book we asked a question, is loving a fact or an abuse? And if it is a fact, is the fact worth the risks? In other words, do we dare open the door to love? In our senior years? Is there a second chance at love? And ultimately, the questions are, am I able to give love and am I capable of receiving it?

Sometimes I think people, seniors especially, have the harder time of it when it comes to receiving love. They're often hesitant to speak love words; they're absolutely lost not knowing how to respond to love words.

Often it boils down to a lack of faith and belief in one's self. Ironic, isn't it. One is burdened with self doubt; someone loving you can blow away the clouds of doubt. One feels inferior; having someone love you makes you the most important person in the world. You wonder if you can face life alone; someone who loves you offers you a partner and a partnership.

If you were to ask me if giving love and/or being the recipient of love is worth the risk, I would say yes. Emphatically. In love, all things are possible.

Including failure. But even that is impossible unless one dares to try. Failure means you did reach out, offered your best self, dreamed new, wonderful dreams, sent your hopes out ahead and tried to reach them, dared when others quit. You opened the door and light shined in. You got rhythm; it was too marvelous for words; perhaps what you found was for all eternity. I hope so, because in all this world there is nothing of more value than the one you love loving you in return.

❦   ❦   ❦

I've been reading a rather sarcastic satire, what the French call a *lampon*. In the seventeenth century during the reign of Charles II, scandalous libel acquired the name lampoon (lampon), literally "let us drink," as in the refrain, "Guzzler, guzzler, my fellow guzzler" followed by a personal attack on some poor soul.

More recently, a lampoon makes fun of someone or something, i.e., one's past history or current activity. Two well known publications, "Mad Magazine" and "The Harvard Lampoon," carry (or carried) lampooning to hilarious heights.

The book I have been reading presents itself as history. Anyone who knows the period being reported howls with laughter. Outrageous understatements and overstatements appeal to my sense of humor. So do good puns, and a proper lampoon is a good pun.

I tried some of the lampooning out on a younger adult who, unless well read, would not have known the period being described. "I didn't know that." "That sheds a whole new light on that." And other such exclamations. She was reading the lampoons as actual history. And, I'm afraid, accepting the exaggerations or the underplayment as gospel truths.

That little experiment reminded me just how carefully we have to choose and use our words, that often what we intend to convey is misinterpreted by the hearer. Or what we hear or read is not at all what the speaker or writer intended.

A man once told me, "She cheated me." I didn't know what he meant, whether he was accusing his partner of having an affair or accusing her of stealing. Fortunately I didn't say anything, just asked him to explain. "She was sick and didn't tell me; she cheated me out of the chance to hold her hand and comfort her; you know, the 'in sickness' part."

I knew what he didn't want to know. Either she didn't want him to see her in her sickly misery or he wasn't important enough in her life for her to seek his comfort. I feared for the latter.

But there's another side to this coin. A man told me once that when he was younger he had suffered a severe spinal injury. There was medical doubt he would walk again, let alone participate in the athletics in which he was skilled. He became very depressed. To make matters worse, he recently had proposed marriage to a young woman and she had accepted.

"The threat was, I would be half a man, crippled. Over time I came to terms with that. What I couldn't deal with was what I would be asking of the girl I loved. Fortunately, the circumstances meant that we were separated, geographically, I mean, and it was some time before she even knew of my injury. When she did, she immediately sent her parents to check on me."

He went on to say that their visit forced him to make the hardest decision he had ever made in his life, before or after. Without mentioning his injury or his depression, he managed to write the young woman a letter, telling her he had second thoughts about their romantic relationship and therefore he was calling it off. She wrote back but he never read the letter.

"I loved her enough to set her free," he said. "My noble gesture."

The trouble was, after months of rehabilitation and more surgery, he was made whole, suffering few lingering negative results of his injury. He said he went from elation to depression and back again, elated that he was physically able and depressed because he had dismissed his loved one so readily.

"She was absolutely wonderful; in a way, I'm still in love with her. But it's not losing her that bugs me. That was my own stupidity and state of mind. What bothers me is that I never gave her a chance to decide. I cheated her of the opportunity to make a choice. I took from her all her rights to make a decision. I thought I was doing her a favor. I wasn't. I was being selfish, stewing in my misery, and when I needed her the most, I shut her out.

"Maybe she would have left anyway. I thought by showing just how much I loved her, proving it by shoving her away, I would solve her doubts. I didn't realize I had diminished her. That realization hurts to this day."

I've thought often of that man's burden. He was right; he made a hard decision, thinking he was doing a noble, loving thing. And he was wrong. Perhaps his girl friend would have broken off their relationship. I don't know. Perhaps she loved him and would have loved him anyway. I don't know that either. What he came to know in time was that loving was a partnership, that decisions are made by two, not one for the other. He had made a decision not his alone to make, and he suffered the emotional consequences all his life.

There's no way of knowing what the young woman felt; no way of knowing if she ever knew the reason for his sudden break off of their promising relationship. What we all know is that undoubtedly she suffered heartbreak and a sense of betrayal. She didn't know, of course, but she had been cheated out of the precious right to make up her own mind. I'm sure she would have found no love in that.

When we think about cheating, naturally we think about infidelity. But there are other ways to cheat someone. Loving is sharing, equal partners, mutual decisions, the *we* I've stressed so heavily. Not sharing the ups and downs, not giving equal status to your partner, making unilateral decisions, replacing *we* with *I* and *you* are all forms of cheating your partner out of his/her rightful role in the partnership. When that's done, there is no meaningful partnership.

❦ ❦ ❦

And a woman told me once, "He doesn't love me; he loves love." And believing that, she shut the man out of her life. I knew the man and I knew differently. I wondered what he had said or done that gave the wrong message.

We can make fun of such bumbling. In a way we would be making fun of ourselves, lampooning our own stumbling and inadequate attempts at love. It's no laughing matter for those disappointed, of course, and our literature is filled with failed love and the devastating consequences which attend failure. Too many talented writers and artists have sunk into despair and depression after revealing their failures; too many took lampon to the serious depths of alcoholism; too many literally ended their lives, an incalculable loss. Two great women poets come to mind: Edna St. Vincent Mallay and Sylvia Plath; one destroyed her life with sex and booze; the other took her life from sheer depression; both penned lines that lift the spirit, a weird combination of death and creation and love and despair.

Which leads to this final thought. Seniors are survivors. We've all lived for well over half a century; some are approaching a full century of life. We have experienced the highs and the lows that living presents. Many have survived inestimable loss; we have persevered. Many (more, I hope) have enjoyed great gifts; we have flourished. We know how to live without sinking, masters of our fate. Of all the things we know, we know that above all else there is the abiding assurance of worth a loved one gives us just by loving us. To seek that someone is not selfish or sinful or the hopeless last thought of a perverted mind. Bent, wrinkled, graying, we disguise the eternally youthful heart beating within us. Old men and old women dream young men and young women's dreams. And we should. No where, except perhaps in modern advertising, is it written that the seniors among us should end their dreaming and give up their search for happiness.

Happiness is singing together when day is
through.

—"Happiness,"
from *You're A Good Man, Charlie Brown,*
Words and Music by Clark Gesner;
New York: Jeremy Music, Inc.
© Jeremy Music, Inc. 1965, 1967.

The Steps of Love

Love   Love, the sublime spirit,
drives our lives: one's heart
exchanged with another,
doubts and fears to outwit.

Discovering   A voice, a glance, a face
fills all your emptiness,
flows to the out most limb,
a wonder time of grace.

Reaching   Reach out, pursue the chance,
offer your best, and if
love be returned, embrace
your partner in love's dance.

Loving   Love with no sense of shame
or regret or remorse.
Love cannot be sullied;
light innocent love's flame.

Banishing   Heed not doubts from yesterday
or future fear. In love
all things are possible;
love provides its own way.

Renouncing   Render to limbo's death
the ego, illusions,
expectations: in love
the death of these is breath.

Planning.   Yield the past to the past;
build on the good, forgive
the bad; rendezvous with
the new day, future vast.

Reality Check Are things what they are?
Is reality what is,
whatever that is,
hot flashes or seminal star?

Committing   Pledge to life. Stand naked
of pretense in your love
as in your lovemaking.
Love is life untainted.

Sharing   Each is of the other,
giving to, taking from.
As entwined strands strengthen
the cord, trust each other.

Relaxing   In love, no power play
intrudes, no guard gates are
erected. Trust excludes
wars and threats of doomsday.

Healing   When hurting, the embrace:
the voiceless touch speaks words
from angels' songs. Doubt and fears
disappear without trace.

Lovemaking With eyes and voice.
Let joys of sight and sound
precede the touch. In
awareness of love rejoice.

Singing   Love itself is a song,
earthy and heavenly
all at once, from one heart
to another. Live long
with me, it sings, and be
what I dreamed from the first:
friend, lover, comforter.
The same is pledged by me.
Let us sing for us two,
not for our yesterdays
but for tomorrow when
love can fulfill anew.

Recommended Reading

The following books are available in many public libraries and through local bookstores as well as online bookstores such as Amazon.com or Barnes & Noble, among others. I've chosen a handful of books worthwhile for seniors, but have omitted most of the popular mass market books.

Health and Sexuality

Chapunoff, Eduardo. *Sex and the Cardiac Patient.* Miami Beach, FL: Bendy Books, 1991.
> *Just what its title says; clear reading for anyone with heart disease, who's had a stroke or is worried about cardiac/vascular issues.*

Crenshaw, Theresa L. *The Alchemy of Love and Lust: Discovering Our Sex Hormones and How They Determine Who We Love, When We Love, and How Often We Love.* New York: Putnam, 1996.
> *More practical and helpful than the title suggests.*

Northrup, Christiane, *Women's Bodies, Women's Wisdom: Creating Physical and Emotional Health and Healing.* Revised and updated. New York: Bantam Books, 1998.
> *A must read for women seeking insight about themselves.*

Pearsall, Paul, *Superimmunity: Master Your Emotions & Improve Your Health.* New York: McGraw-Hill,. 1987.
> *Argues that sexual activity increases health, especially by strengthening the immune system.*

Shabsigh, Ridwan. *Back to Great Sex: Overcome Erectile Dysfunction and Reclaim Lost Intimacy.* New York: Kensington, 2002.
> *Deals with erectile dysfunction, physical and emotional. Very helpful.*

Doress–Waters, Paula, and Diana Laskin Siegal. *The New Ourselves, Growing Older: Women Aging With Knowledge and Power.* New York: Simon & Schuster, 1994.
Published in cooperation with the Boston Women's Health Book Collective; illustrations by Roselaine Perkis. An important book.

Touch

Hooper, Anne. *Anne Hooper's Ultimate Sex Guide: A Therapist's Guide to the Programs and Techniques That Will Enhance Your Relationship and Transform Your Life.* Revised edition. New York: Dorling Kindersley, 2001.
The title is somewhat misleading; although sensual touch might lead to sexual touching, the need to touch and be touched is primary.

Lovemaking:

Altman, Alan M., and Laurie Ashner. *Making Love the Way We Used To—Or Better: Secrets To Satisfying Midlife Sexuality.* Lincolnwood, IL: Contemporary Books, 2001.
Help for older people.

Barbach, Lonnie. *50 Ways to Please Your Lover (While You Please Yourself).* New York: Dutton, 1997.
Mutual pleasure and satisfaction is an important goal of lovemaking.

General

Kemp, Edith Ankersmit, and Jerrold E. Kemp. *Older Couples, New Romances: Finding & Keeping Love in Later Life,* rev. ed. Berkeley, CA: Celestial Arts, 2002.
Inerviews with senior couples. Very practical, scientific, and useful information.

Healthgate. *www.rowan.org* or *www.healthgate.com.* A website that provides information on aging, sexuality, and health. One may access the information without charge simply by going on line. The site deals with such questions as "Is sex good for you?" and "Can your heart handle sex?" and "How much sex do older people have?" The site also deals with specific senior issues having to do with illnesses, disabilities, and sex. Health-gate is a resource worth exploring. The sites are sponsored by Rowan Medical Center, Salisbury, NC. Click on "Your Health." The vast information may be accessed also through local hospitals. Click on "Services/Programs" or "Health-Fields."

Pearlman, Mickey, ed., A *Few Thousand Words About Love*. New York, St. Martin's Press, 1998.
An anthology by seventeen people, some of whom you will know; beautifully written—even if you don't believe in love.

Scott, Susan. *Create the Love of Your Life*. New York: Kensington, 1993.
Just what the title suggests.

Solot, Dorian, and Marshall Miller. *Unmarried to Each Other: The Essential Guide to Living Together as an Unmarried Couple*. New York: Marlowe, 2002.
Practical, humorous, real life stuff.

Smalley, Gary. *Secrets to Lasting Love: Uncovering the Keys to Life-Long Intimacy*. New York: Simon & Schuster, 2000.
There are no secrets, really, just practice, but if you think there are secrets, some might be revealed in this reference.